D0297727

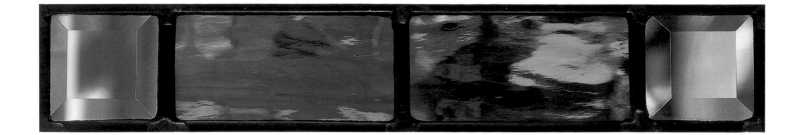

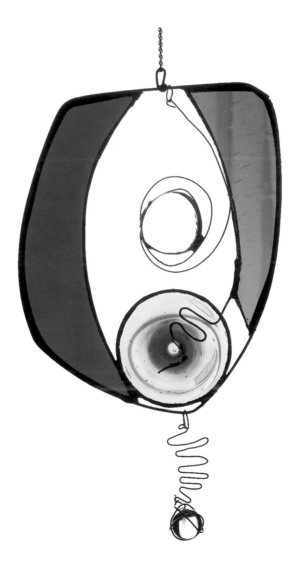

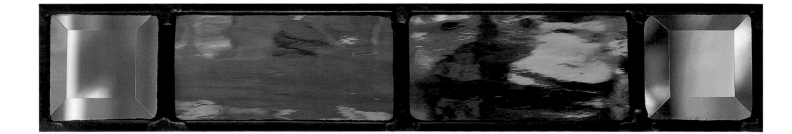

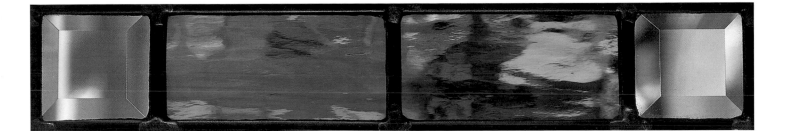

Stained Glass

IN A WEEKEND

Stylish designs and practical projects

LYNETTE WRIGLEY

NEW HOLLAND

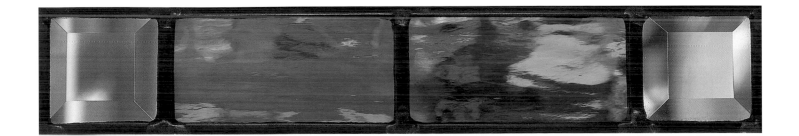

For Mary

First published in 1999 by
New Holland Publishers (UK) Ltd
London · Cape Town · Sydney · Auckland

24 Nutford Place
London W1H 6DQ
United Kingdom

80 McKenzie Street
Cape Town 8001
South Africa

Level 1, Unit 4,
14 Aquatic Drive
Frenchs Forest, NSW 2086
Australia

Unit 1A, 218 Lake Road
Northcote
Auckland
New Zealand

10 9 8 7 6 5 4 3 2 1

ISBN 1 85974 090 1

Editor: Gillian Haslam
Editorial Assistant: Kate Latham
Designer: Peter Crump
Photographer: Shona Wood

Managing Editor: Coral Walker

Reproduction by cmyk pre-press (Pty) Ltd
Printed and bound by Times Offset (M) Sdn. Bhd

Every effort has been made to present clear and accurate instructions.
Therefore, the author and publishers can accept no liability for any
injury, illness or damage which may inadvertently be caused to the
user while following these instructions.

All designs illustrated are for private and personal use only or to be used
as a source of inspiration. They are not to be used for commercial gain
or commercial purposes.

CONTENTS

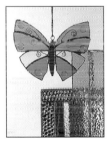

INTRODUCTION

Anyone who has encountered the beautiful stained glass windows displayed in cathedrals and churches will have marvelled at the glorious colours of the glass and the skill of the craftsmen. Today, more and more people are discovering this skill for themselves.

Along with ceramics, jewellery, silk painting and many other crafts, stained glass is now a regular fixture on the craft scene. It is to be found for sale in craft markets, on the syllabus at college, and displayed in exhibitions and galleries. Stained glass is now not only a medium used for creating windows but also for all manner of decorative objects, from lightcatchers to mirrors and from jewellery to sculpture. In this book there are examples of just a few of the many ideas that are possible, showing the versatility that glass can offer.

As well as showing the traditional method of assembling a window with lead, I have also included step-by-step descriptions of how to work with copper foil and contemporary applications such as appliqué. Etching has also become a popular look for decorative glassware and there are some simple methods provided for creating this effect.

Copper foiling has become one of the most popular methods of assembling glass in recent years and its versatility allows you to create a variety of decorative household objects with glass, especially three-dimensional ones. This is sometimes known as the Tiffany technique after the American Louis Comfort Tiffany who, in the late nineteenth century, changed the way stained glass looked and the way it was made. His craftsmen in the Tiffany studios found traditional lead was too inflexible to handle tiny pieces of glass. Instead, they wrapped each piece of glass in a thin strip of copper before assembling and soldering. This enabled them to make highly detailed and intricate designs in glass, especially the famous lamps, synonymous with Tiffany's name.

Copper foil has contributed to the popularity of stained glass today as it is an easy technique to master at home and is useful for so many projects, from small boxes to complete windows. Glass artists often use up pieces of glass left over from large window commissions in this way, making smaller items to sell in shops and markets.

Stained glass can offer a fascinating and rewarding hobby and is now more accessible than ever for those wishing to take up this absorbing craft. Most suppliers offer excellent mail order services for those living too far to visit their nearest stockist.

If you have never cut a piece of glass before, do not be daunted. While teaching weekend workshops on stained glass, I am constantly inspired by people's creativity. Once they realise it is not so difficult, their enthusiasm is boundless. There is a magic to stained glass which becomes irresistible when you begin working with it. Once you have mastered the simple techniques of cutting glass, your confidence will grow and the ideas will flow.

GETTING STARTED

This chapter describes the various tools and materials required for stained glass and explains the basic techniques which are used in the projects that follow. Read this chapter carefully before you begin and refer back to it when making the projects for more detailed instructions on techniques such as cutting glass or applying copper foil. It is also a good idea to practise some of these techniques on scrap glass in order to build up your skill and confidence. Once you have mastered these techniques, you will be able to adapt the projects given here and make your own unique pieces.

EQUIPMENT AND MATERIALS

As is the case with many crafts, when you take up a new hobby you will probably need to invest a little money in a few specialized tools and materials. Many of the items listed here are relatively inexpensive and will last you a lifetime. Most of the suppliers listed at the back of the book provide catalogues and offer mail order services, so don't be deterred if you do not have a stained glass supplier in your town. You can also check your telephone directory for local outlets.

The equipment and materials listed on the right are all explained in detail on the following pages.

Jewellery findings are used in some of the smaller projects, such as the mobiles or the glass pendant. These, and jewellery pliers, are also available by mail order from the suppliers listed at the back of the book or from craft suppliers.

Please read the safety notes on page 19 thoroughly before you begin work on any of the projects.

Scraps of glass to practise cutting
Glass cutter and cutting oil
Cutting square
Grozing pliers
Carborundum stone
Soldering iron and stand
Solder
Flux
Tip cleaner
Copper foil
Patina
Rubber gloves
Lead cames
Lead vice and lead knife
Horseshoe nails
Lead light cement
Dustpan and brush
Safety goggles
Fire grate blackener
Etching cream or spray

WORK SURFACE
You can work on any steady table with an even surface with plenty of space around you. If it is not a workbench, cover the tabletop with plenty of newspaper to protect its surface. When cutting glass, use thick paper or felt to cover the table. Always keep a dustpan and brush handy and sweep up the thin slivers of glass frequently.

GLASS CUTTERS
My advice is to invest in the best type of cutter available and there are now some very good ones on the market.
• **CARBIDE STEEL WHEEL CUTTER:** this is most commonly used cutter. The hard cutting wheel can be replaced when it becomes blunt and the end of the handle is fashioned into a ball shape used for tapping the scored glass. Cutting oil is required to prolong the wheel's life, so keep a jar with a cotton pad soaked in oil and occasionally dip the wheel into it.
• **TUNGSTEN CARBIDE WHEEL CUTTER:** this cutter often has a built-in oil reservoir and is very comfortable to hold. If you are a beginner, you can achieve good results relatively quickly with this type of cutter.
• **PISTOL GRIP CUTTER:** this is the same type of tool as the tungsten carbide wheel cutter but with an unusual shape for a preferred grip.

CUTTING SQUARE
This is used to score straight lines and to make sure that right angles are precise.

PLIERS
Several different types of pliers are used in stained glass work.
• **GROZING PLIERS:** these pliers have curved serrated jaws designed for gripping glass and are perfect for both breaking glass and removing small irregular bits from the edges of glass. They are also known as grozer breakers.
• **RUNNING PLIERS:** these are plastic or metal pliers designed for breaking long thin strips of glass.

SOLDERING IRON
Soldering is the method of joining two sections of metal together where they meet. This is done with a soldering

CUTTING

Safety goggles

Running pliers

Pistol grip cutter

Tungsten carbide wheel cutter

Oil filler

Snips

Carbide steel wheel cutter

Scalpel

Grozing pliers

Cutting square

SOLDERING

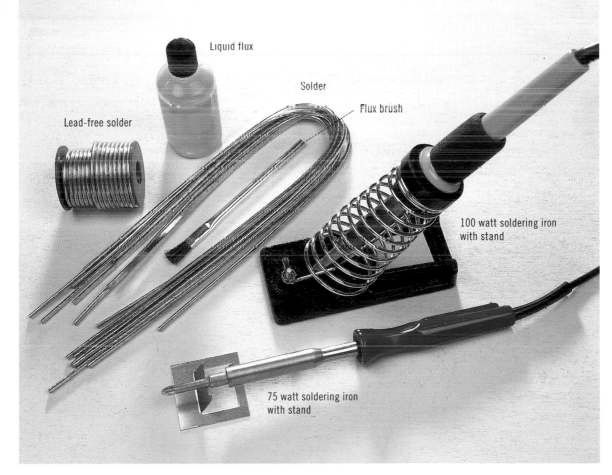

Liquid flux

Solder

Lead-free solder

Flux brush

100 watt soldering iron with stand

75 watt soldering iron with stand

COPPER FOILING

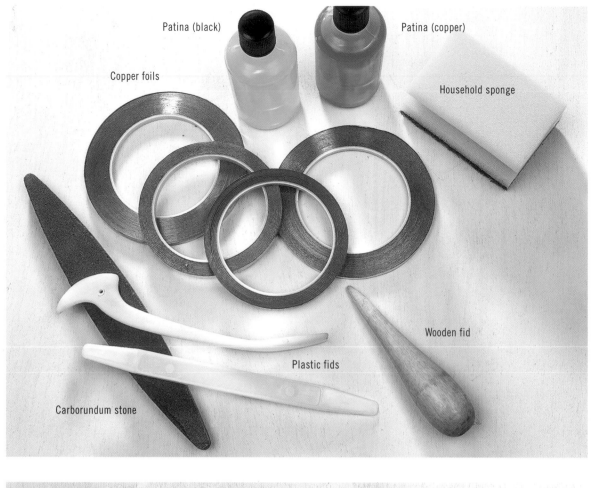

Patina (black)

Patina (copper)

Copper foils

Household sponge

Wooden fid

Plastic fids

Carborundum stone

LEADING

Horseshoe nails

Lead vice

Whiting

Lightweight hammer

Tallow candle

Lead knife

Lead cames

Cement brush

Fire grate blackener

Wire brush

Lead light cement

iron. You need to use a soldering iron with a minimum wattage of 75 watts. There are several types available from 75 watts up to 200 watts. The most commonly used iron is one of 100 watts. Always use an iron stand to rest the hot iron on and turn it off when you leave the room or no longer need to use it.

SOLDER
Solder is available in sticks or lengths. It is a combination of tin and lead. The mix can be 50/50 (tin/lead) or 60/40 (tin/lead). The latter has a lower melting point and will flow more easily, producing a more pronounced silvery finish. Lead-free solder is also available in 500 g (1 lb) rolls. You may prefer to use this when making jewellery.

FLUX
Flux is necessary to allow the melted solder to flow while bonding the two materials together. It is available as a liquid or paste for copper foil work and as a solid substance called tallow candle for lead work.

TIP CLEANER
A soldering iron will accumulate deposits on the tips. Although a damp sponge is useful for occasionally wiping the tip on, there is a chemical tip cleaner which will remove the deposits easily, making the iron work more efficiently.

CARBORUNDUM STONE
This natural stone files away sharp edges on glass and is used before wrapping the edge of the glass in copper foil.

COPPER FOIL
Copper foil is supplied as a tape which comes in pre-cut rolls in a variety of widths. It is also available with a black or silver backing. A wider foil will result in a wider seam (join) and a narrow foil a more delicate seam between the pieces of glass once they have been soldered. It is used to cover the edges of the pieces of glass which are then assembled and soldered together. It is extremely versatile and useful for small or larger projects, especially three-dimensional ones.

PATINA
Available in liquid form, this changes the colour of solder from silver to grey/black or a copper tone. Applied with a sponge when the project is complete, it must then be washed off with water and detergent. Always wear rubber gloves when using this product.

FID
This is a plastic or wooden implement used to smooth down the copper foil around the edges of glass before soldering. It is also used to prise apart the channels of the lead cames.

LEAD CAMES
These strips of lead have a channel on each side for accommodating the glass. They come in lengths of 1.7 m (6 ft) and in a variety of widths.

LEAD VICE
Before use, lead cames must be stretched to straighten out any kinks. One end is clamped in the vice, which must be fixed to a surface, while the other end is held with pliers and pulled. If you don't have a lead vice, you can straighten the cames by pulling them with the help of another person – simply clamp the ends with pliers and pull.

LEAD KNIFE
This is a knife with a curved blade designed for cutting lead cames.

HORSESHOE NAILS
The flat sides of these nails are perfect for holding glass in position while making a panel using lead cames.

LEAD LIGHT CEMENT
This is a specialized fast-drying putty for leaded windows. Whiting (a chalk-like powder) is used to dry excess cement and clean the glass after cementing.

FIRE GRATE BLACKENER
This darkens the cames. Apply to the last brushing of the cames, after the whiting and cement are brushed off.

ETCHING CREAM OR SPRAY
This creates an effect similar to sandblasting. See the projects on pages 32 and 50 for more details.

GLASS

When you first look through a catalogue from a stained glass supplier, the choice of glass can be bewildering. There are many different types and colours to choose from. If possible, it is best to visit a stockist and select the colours yourself. Once you become familiar with the types and colours available, ordering from a catalogue will be easier.

MACHINE-MADE
This term refers to glass which is made by machine rather than by hand. When the glass is in a hot liquid state it is rolled out onto a metal surface. There are many types of machine-made glass, the following are a few examples.
- **CATHEDRAL GLASS:** this has an even surface texture and is easy to cut. Ideal for beginners.
- **STREAKY GLASS:** two or more colours are swirled together in one piece of glass
- **WATER GLASS:** glass with an even, wavy appearance on the surface.
- **SEMI-ANTIQUE GLASS:** this has a distinct surface pattern of tiny striations. An easy glass to cut and useful for beginners.
- **IRIDIZED GLASS:** glass with an iridescent shine on the surface.
- **OPALESCENT GLASS:** most opals are machine-made. It is characterized by its opacity as opposed to the other machine-made glasses which are transparent. For this reason it has been used extensively for lamp-making. It comes in many colours and a variety of densities.

ANTIQUE GLASS
This name refers to glass which is blown by mouth as opposed to machine-made. The name does not refer to the age of the glass but the centuries' old technique by which it is made. Glass is blown into a long cylinder. The ends are removed and a cut is made in the side. It is then re-heated and folded out into a flat sheet. Because it is hand-made there are irregularities in the glass which make each sheet unique.

GLASS ACCESSORIES

ROUNDELS
Machine-pressed or hand-spun circles of glass with smooth edges. Available in a variety of sizes.

BEVELS
Glass shapes with smooth bevelled edges. Available in different sizes.

NUGGETS
These resemble flattened glass marbles. They are available in a range of stunning colours and various sizes.

CUTTING GLASS

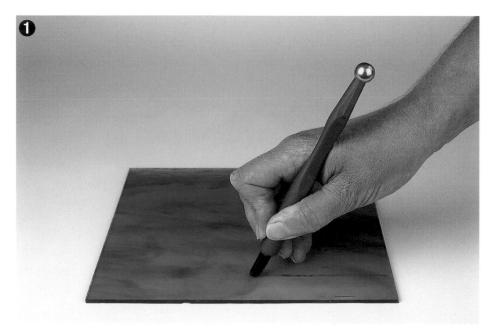

Cutting glass is much easier than people think. With practice you will gain confidence and this is the most important step in this craft. Before you let yourself loose on coloured glass, try to practise as much as you can on ordinary inexpensive 2 or 3 mm (⅛ in) window glass. Always wear safety glasses when cutting glass.

The way you hold the cutter depends on the type you are using and, to a certain extent, how comfortable it feels. You need to be able to exert pressure and to see the cutting wheel as you push the cutter across the surface of the glass ①.

You will find that using your free hand to steady the cutter and add extra pressure will also help ②.

The mark you make with the wheel of the cutter is called a 'score'. You will both see and 'hear' this score being made if you are applying enough pressure. Make some scores on scrap glass first. Start the score from one side of the glass and apply pressure as you push it across to the other. You can start the score just inside the edge of the glass and release the pressure just 1 mm (1/16 in) before you reach the other edge. **Do not go over a score a second time.** It ruins the cutter and will not help the first score to work. Push the cutter forward and away from you.

If you are following the lines of a pattern, place the paper pattern beneath the glass.

You must always continue a score from one edge of the glass to the other. A piece of glass will break just where it wants and not where you want if you end a score in the middle of the glass. Use pieces of glass not too much bigger than the shape you want to cut. If necessary, cut the glass down first so that it is closer in size to the shape you need, but still leave enough of a margin for you to hold and break the glass with fingers or pliers. Photos ③④⑤⑥ show how to score and cut a shape from a sheet of glass.

BREAKING GLASS

You will know if you have applied the correct pressure when you come to break the pieces of glass apart. To break the glass apart you can use your hands if the piece is big enough. Place your thumbs either side of the score with your fingers curled into your palms underneath. Always hold the glass next to the score. Grip the glass firmly and snap the glass apart ⑦.

You can also use pliers. Hold the glass in one hand and, with the other hand, place the head of the pliers next to the score. Using the same movement, snap the glass apart ⑧. Some glass breaks more easily than others. With experience you will learn how different types of glass behave when scoring and breaking .

❸

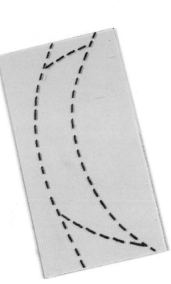

❹

❺

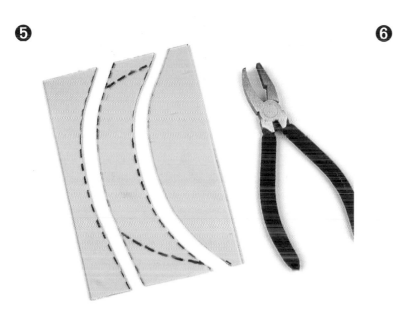

❻

❼

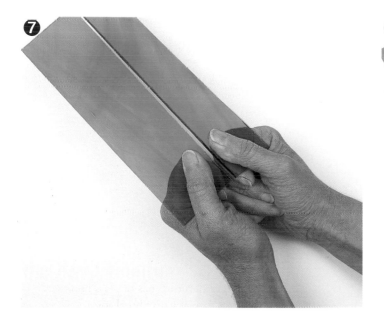

❽

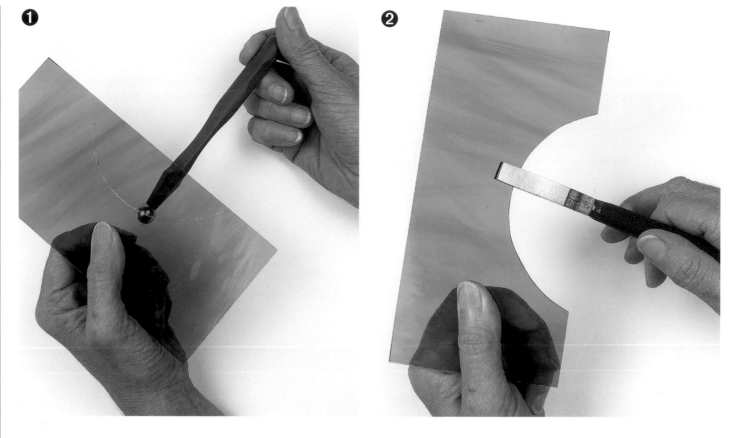

TAPPING

To encourage a stubborn or brittle piece of glass to break, tap the glass underneath with the ball end of the glass cutter. You must tap under the score line. You will see how the score changes in appearance as it fractures. Always hold the glass very firmly to keep it still while tapping. Tapping is sometimes essential when trying to break open a score that follows the shape of a curve ①.

GROZING

You may sometimes be left with little jagged bits of glass on the edge of the cut piece. You can nip these off using the grozing pliers. 'Bite' or grip these pieces with the jaws of the pliers and carefully but firmly snap off.

The pliers are serrated inside the jaws. Use these to remove thin slivers from the edge of the glass. Place the jaws of the pliers over the edge of the glass and close gently. Roll the pliers backwards and downwards to remove these sharp slivers ②.

CUTTING STRAIGHT LINES

Using a cutting square is essential for obtaining a clean, straight line. It can take a little practice to get used to using it but it is worth the effort. Place the cutting square on the glass and press very firmly on it with one hand.

Holding the cutter with the other hand, start at the top and place the cutter next to the square. Apply pressure and bring the cutter down towards you and along the edge of the square. The secret is to remember to apply pressure to the cutting square and to keep it steady while you press and pull the glass cutter towards you ③.

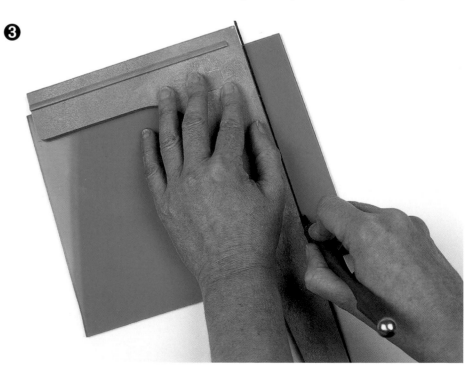

CUTTING CIRCLES

There are special glass cutters for scoring a perfect circle of a certain size. However, as you will mainly be using a hand-held glass cutter, here is a very straightforward method.

Either draw the circle directly onto the glass with a felt-tipped pen or place the glass over paper with a circle drawn on. Leave a margin of glass around the circle and start the score from one edge of the glass. When you arrive at the circle, start to follow the curve for a short distance and then move off to the side of the glass. Place your cutter back on the circle at the point where you left and move further around the curve, continuing to move off to the edge of the glass ④.

To break the curve, use the ball end of the cutter to tap underneath the score to help release the glass. Use pliers to break off the unwanted pieces of glass, removing one piece at a time ⑤.

Finally, neaten the edges of the circle with the grozing pliers, removing any sharp angles, aiming for a smooth continuous curve ⑥.

SMOOTHING EDGES

Sharp edges and points of glass can be removed by rubbing along a carborundum stone ⑦. It is especially helpful before copper foiling. Prevent dust forming by keeping the stone wet as you work. You can also smooth glass on wet and dry abrasive paper. Electric grinding machines, although more expensive than a carborundum stone, are also used for grinding edges and changing the shape of glass. Always wear safety glasses.

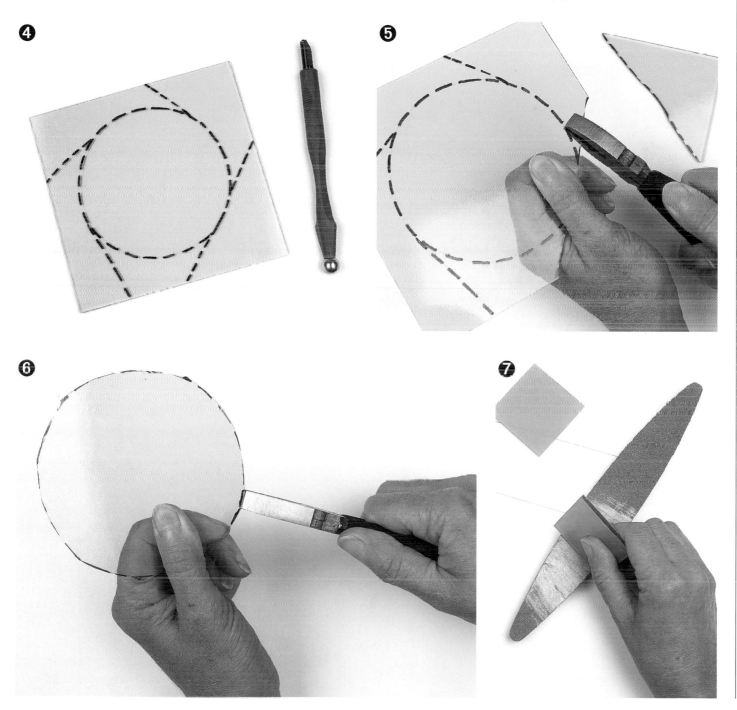

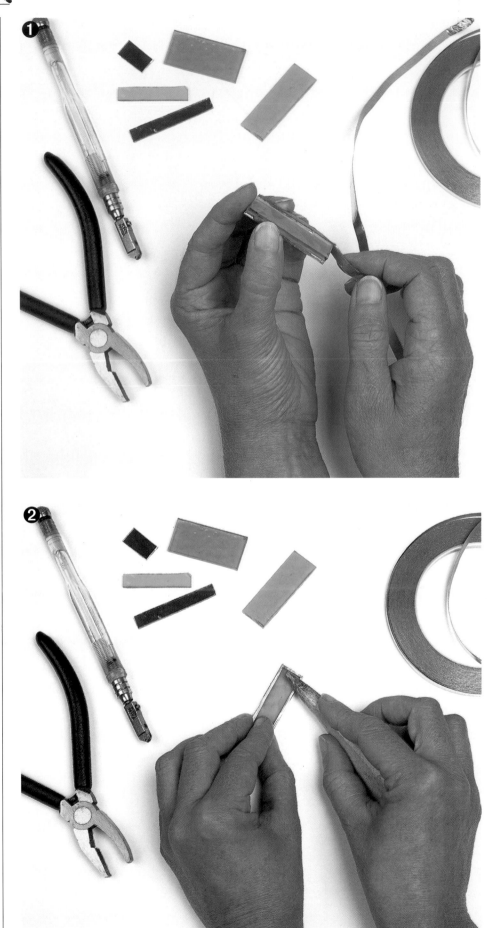

APPLYING COPPER FOIL TO GLASS

This method of assembling glass is especially useful for working with small pieces of glass and three-dimensional objects. The adhesive side of the foil is pressed firmly to the edges of the glass, then all pieces are assembled and soldered together.

Cut the glass to size so that it butts up to the adjacent piece with no large gaps, then wash and dry it to remove any dust. Pull back the protective paper and centre the edge of the glass on the foil. Leave an even amount of foil exposed on each side. Overlap the foil slightly where you began. Make sure the tape is even and you cannot see the overlap ①.

Now fold the excess or exposed foil onto the sides of the glass and press down. Use a fid to smooth the foil along the edges and sides ②.

SOLDERING

You must apply flux before soldering copper-foiled glass as it allows the solder to flow. Flux should be applied with a brush ③.

There are three different stages or types of soldering. Switch the soldering iron on and wait for it to heat up before you begin.

A) TACKING

Once all your glass is in position you don't want to risk any movement during soldering. Apply flux in several key areas (where pieces meet) and melt a small amount of solder – just enough to hold everything in place. These blobs will be smoothed out later when you are soldering the seams ④.

B) TINNING

Tinning is an essential stage and holds the piece together. It refers to a thin layer of solder which is applied after the flux to all the seams of foiled glass and is enough to hold the glass together. A thin layer of solder is usually sufficient on the unseen areas such as the back or inside of a project ⑤.

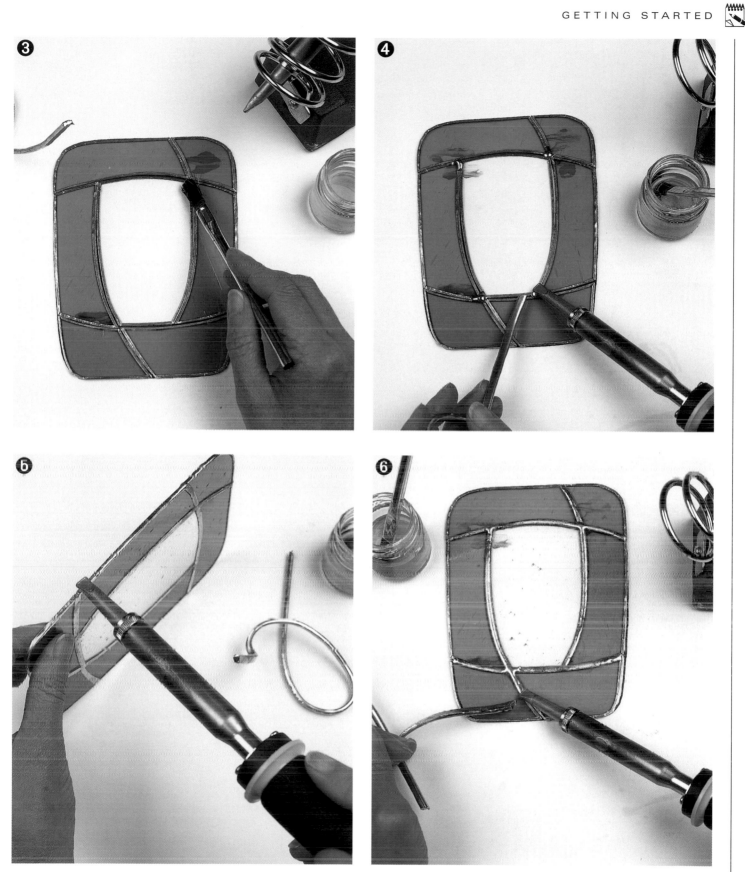

C) BEAD SOLDERING

To create a nicer finish for the front of your project, you can bead solder. On all the seams where two pieces of foiled glass join, apply the flux and enough solder to 'raise' the amount of solder into a smooth rounded 'bead'. Remember to keep applying the flux and to use a steady hand to move the tip of the soldering iron very slowly down the copper-foiled seams of the glass for a smooth finish. The solder will melt when you hold it next to the iron and a smooth rounded seam will develop if you work slowly and with care. Keep the tip of your iron clean by wiping it on a damp sponge whenever deposits build up ⑥.

WASHING COPPER-FOILED PROJECTS

After completing the soldering on copper-foiled projects, always wash the piece with warm soapy water. The flux is mildly corrosive and the project will then be ready for a patina if you choose to use one. Apply the patina wearing rubber gloves and then wash the project once again.

WORKING WITH LEAD

Lead cames come in a variety of widths and in lengths of around 1.7 m (6 feet). Unlike copper foil it has a 'heart' in the centre. When you cut glass for leaded projects you must allow for this 'heart' and leave a gap between each piece of glass. The heart of the lead may vary in size but is usually 2 mm (1/16 in). Lead cames have an empty channel down each side where the glass will slot in. Before working with the lead it must be stretched. Use a lead vice to grip one end while holding the other with pliers and pulling until the lead is straight with no kinks. Alternatively, ask a friend to help by pulling one end while you hold the other (see page 11).

CUTTING THE LEAD

The lead is cut into the desired lengths with a lead knife. Place the knife on the top of the lead and rock it from side to side as you also press down gently ①.

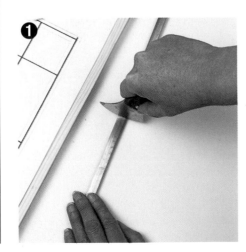

It can be crushed easily if you apply pressure too quickly or use a blunt knife. Some distortion is inevitable, but you can use a fid to open a channel.

SOLDERING THE LEAD TOGETHER

A leaded panel only requires solder at the junctions where one piece of lead meets another. Apply flux to each joint or intersection before you solder. The flux used for lead is tallow candle. Rub each joint with the tallow candle. Hold a piece of solder over the joint and allow a small amount to adhere to the lead beneath by melting it with the iron ②. Take great care and only hold the iron on the lead for a few seconds. If you take longer you will melt the lead itself and be left with a hole. You only need enough solder to form a small flat blob.

CEMENTING

When the leaded panel is complete you must cement it for extra strength and also for weather proofing. The process not only cleans the glass but darkens the cames as well. Use a small scrubbing brush and push the cement under all the cames where the glass has slotted in ③.

Do one side first and sprinkle with some whiting powder, then rub over the panel. Turn over the panel and prepare the other side in the same way. Leave the panel for around half an hour depending on the weather. If it is warm and the cement dries too fast it will be difficult to clean off the excess.

Use a plastic or wooden fid to draw the excess cement from around the cames. Scrub the panel on both sides with a clean small scrubbing brush. Check for any cement left that has

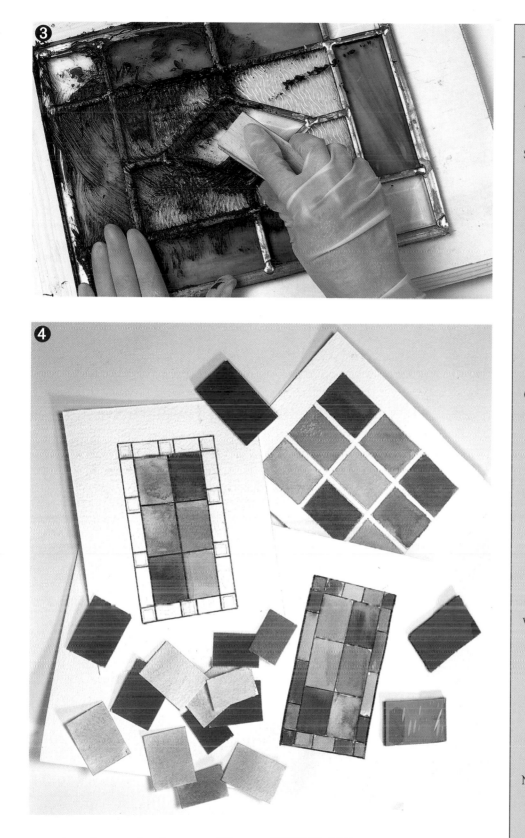

❸

❹

seeped out from under the cames. The whiting also helps to clean the glass as you push the brush across the glass and the cames. The more you brush, the darker the lead cames will become.

If you wish to darken the cames with fire grate blackener, apply a small amount and continue brushing.

PATTERNS

Once you become familiar with making stained glass, you'll want to create your own designs. Try creating small watercolours first or cut out pieces of coloured paper and make collages ④.

PROJECTS AND GALLERIES
FOR STAINED GLASS

SUNFLOWER APPLIQUÉ

Appliqué offers great freedom with designs and can be absolutely compelling. This technique is similar to making a mosaic – the pieces are glued to a panel of clear glass and then grouted to fill the areas between the coloured glass. A glass picture or window panel can be created using this technique with fragments of glass, by cutting glass to a specified design or by a combination of both. This sunflower used up both large and small pieces of scrap (or cullet) glass I had left over from a larger window.

1 First cut the petals from larger pieces of glass. Lay the yellow glass over the first copy of the pattern and score the petal shape with the cutter, following the lines below. Press hard with the cutter and maintain an even pressure, guiding the wheel along the line and moving from one side of the glass to the other. Break apart with grozing pliers or tap from underneath if you have difficulty breaking the glass.

YOU WILL NEED

Pattern (see page 70) – you will need two copies of the pattern

Assorted offcuts of glass in shades of yellow, brown and pale and medium green, or colours of your choice

Glass cutter

Grozing pliers

4 mm (³/₁₆ in) clear glass, cut to approximately 30 x 30 cm (12 x 12 in)

Glass bond glue (from a hardware shop)

Tweezers

Household filler

Black universal stainer

Bowl and plastic spatula

Protective gloves

Sponge

TIP

You can build up a palette of colours by collecting small pieces of glass that would otherwise be discarded. Store them in boxes according to their colour in preparation for a panel or project using this technique.

2 Clean the square of clear glass thoroughly, then place over the second pattern. Arrange some of the cut pieces together on the clear glass and decide how the colours look together. Use a few shades of yellow and intersperse some brown or other colour of your choice. Glue the petals in place. Put plenty of glue around the edge of each piece and a little in the middle and carefully lay on the glass.

3 Wait for the glue to start to set so the petals will not slide around on the glass square. Meanwhile, cut some small pieces in shades of green in preparation for the background. They do not have to be a specific shape – you can make random scores and break the pieces apart using the pliers. Save any small pieces for the centre, or use them to fill in gaps.

4 Gluing can be messy so use the tweezers to lay down or remove the tiny pieces. You can flood the central area by applying the glue straight onto the clear glass and laying the tiny pieces down on it. Fill the central area mainly with the brown glass, with just a few touches of yellow and green. Also fill and glue the outer areas of the panel, then leave the panel to set (this can take up to 24 hours).

5 Once the whole panel has set, fill in the gaps with filler. In a bowl mix some black stainer into the filler. Don't make it too wet. Wearing protective gloves, use a plastic spatula to spread the filler across the panel, slowly allowing it to fill the gaps between the glass. Then, with a very slightly dampened sponge, wipe over the filler to help it fill the gaps and remove it from the glass surface. When you are happy with the results, allow the panel to dry. You can then carefully clean any excess filler from the panel.

BLUE GALLERY

Circular hanging
Made from opalescent and cathedral glass, this is assembled in the same way as the project on page 36.

Candlestick
The candle holder sitting atop this attractive glass stand is a lampshade cap, tinned and stained with patina.

Pyramid box
The clear outer box and the blue pyramid are assembled separately, then soldered together.
Richard Scowen

Silver mirror

Coloured glass and a diamond bevel
have been silvered, assembled with
copper foil and edged with lead.
Anji Marfleet

Appliqué vase

Strips of coloured glass have been filed
and stuck to a plain vase with U.V. glue.

CANDLE CUBE

One of the many decorative techniques that artists use in a stained glass window is etching or sandblasting. There is a new product now available that is very convenient to use and, although not as durable, it will give a similar effect. It comes in the form of a spray and coats the surface of the glass almost like a paint. For a decorative frosted effect, I have used it on a piece of pale blue cathedral glass which not only enriches the colour but also hides the metal base of the nightlight.

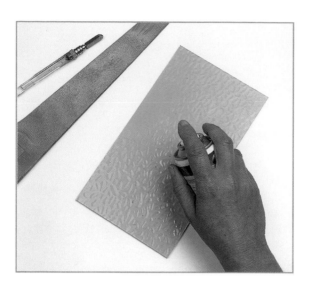

1 Carefully read the manufacturer's instructions printed on the spray can and follow the precautions. Clean the glass and spray with a light, even coat on the lightly textured side. Leave to dry for at least 1 hour.

YOU WILL NEED

Pale blue cathedral glass, approximately 30 x 30 cm (12 x 12 in)
Spray etch
Sheet of white paper
Pen
Ruler
Cutting square
Glass cutter
Grozing pliers
Carborundum stone
Drinking glasses (used in step 4 to prop up the sides of the cube)
Optical glue (ultraviolet)
Silver-plated wire
Jewellery pliers
Nightlight

TIP

The spray etch and the optical glue are available from stained glass suppliers. The silver plated wire and the jewellery pliers are available from bead shops.

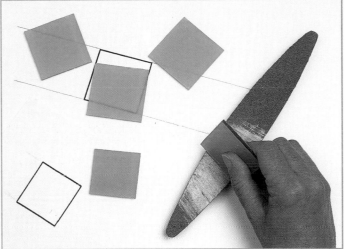

2 Cut strips of the glass first. Cut on the smooth side of the glass which is not etched. Draw a perfect square 5 x 5 cm (2 x 2 in) on the paper and extend the lines on two facing sides (this can be seen more clearly in the photo for step 3). Place the glass on top of the paper. Use the extended lines on the paper to line up the cutting square. Hold the cutting square down firmly so it does not slip. With the other hand, place the glass cutter next to the cutting square at the top of the glass, press down and pull steadily towards you without letting the cutting square move.

3 Break this strip apart using grozing pliers, lay it back on the pattern and cut again into a square following the same method. Cut four squares in total. Draw another square for the base – this should be 2 mm (⅛ in) shorter and narrower. Cut a piece of glass to this size. Gently rub the cut edges of the glass squares on the carborundum stone to blunt the glass and remove any sharp splinters. Do not rub too vigorously or you will fracture the edges.

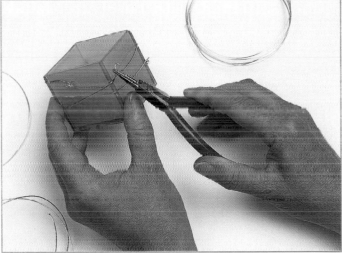

4 Find something suitable to act as a prop for the cube while the glue sets (I used drinking glasses). Practice first. Lay some glue along one edge of each piece of glass and place it carefully next to the side of the other. The etched sides should be on the inside of the cube. Prop the sides to make sure they stay upright and at right angles to each other. When the first two sides have been glued together, glue all four edges of the bottom piece and slip into place. Now glue and place the remaining two side pieces in position. Leave the cube to set for at least ten hours without touching it.

5 Cut some lengths of silver wire long enough to wrap about one and a half times around the cube. Using the jewellery pliers, twist the ends into tight spirals. Wrap the wire around the box at angles, using the jewellery pliers to tie and twist the ends together. Add a nightlight and you have a pretty dinner table candle container.

DECORATIVE GLASS PANEL

This stained glass panel looks stunning hanging in a window to catch the light or as the central panel in a cupboard door. The panel measures 31 x 19.5 cm (12½ x 7⅜ in), but you can easily change the dimensions of the pattern to suit the size of your cupboard.

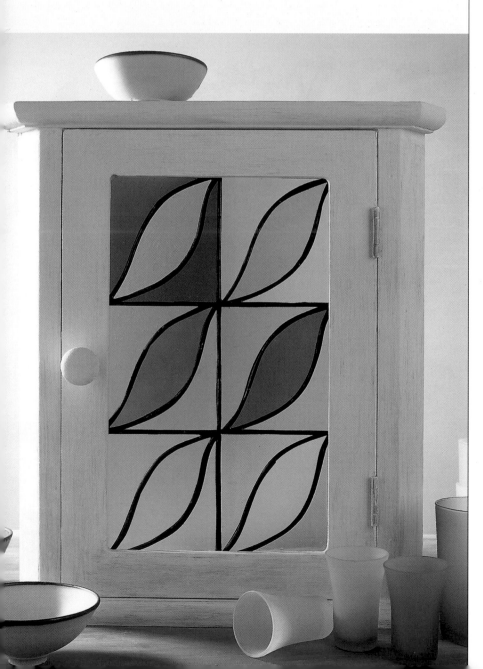

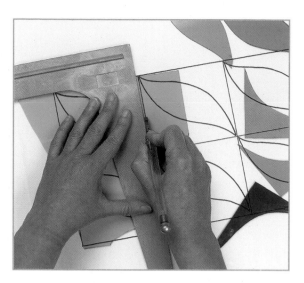

1 First, cut the straight edges of glass. Lay the glass on top of the paper pattern and line up the straight edge with the side of one of the boxes. Starting from the edge of the glass, line up the side of the glass cutter against the straight edge of the cutting square. Press the square firmly to keep it in position. Pull the cutter towards you with steady, even pressure. Break the glass along the scored line, using pliers if necessary.

YOU WILL NEED

Pattern (see page 71)
Large sheet of white paper
Fine black felt-tipped pen
Semi-antique glass in five colours, 15 cm² (½ sq ft) of each
Cutting square
Glass cutter
Pliers
Carborundum stone
6 mm (¼ in) black-backed copper foil
Plastic or wooden fid (or a pencil)
Flux and brush
Solder (4-5 sticks)
Soldering iron
Black-it patina
Sponge
Gloves

--- TIP ---

If adapting this design for a cupboard door, use the existing glass or wooden inner door panel as a pattern to ensure you make the piece to the correct size.

2 Place the glass back on the paper, aligning it precisely with the pattern outlines. To cut the curves, start from the edge of the glass and push the cutter along the line of the pattern. Keep a steady pressure and continue to the end of the line.

3 Hold the glass firmly in one hand and place the pliers next to the scored line. Grip the glass firmly with the pliers and carefully separate the two pieces of glass. To help release the glass, you can tap gently underneath the score with the end of the cutter. Continue to cut all the pieces of glass in this way.

4 Rub the cut edges on the carborundum stone to remove any sharp slivers. Wash the glass in warm, soapy water and then dry. Place each piece of glass in the centre of a length of copper foil so that equal amounts of foil appear on each side. (Here, black foil has been used as the solder will be coloured with a black patina in step 6.) Overlap the foil slightly at the join. Fold the foil over the sides of the glass and smooth down with a fid or pencil.

5 Lay the glass back in position on the paper pattern. Brush the foil with flux and tack solder into position. Bead solder all the seams properly, then turn the panel over and tin solder the back and sides. Wash the panel carefully in warm, soapy water.

6 Wearing protective gloves, apply the liquid patina with a sponge. Make sure you cover all the silver solder. Turn the panel over and apply the patina to the back and sides. There will not be any copper showing through as black-backed tape has been used. Wash the panel again in warm, soapy water, then rinse in clean water.

PRESSED LEAF MIRROR

Dried leaves or flowers are very decorative and are especially useful to those who like to make their own greetings cards. I often open books to find leaves fluttering onto the carpet from a collection made during the autumn. If leaves have not kept their colour I spray them with gold paint. In this project I have combined a variety of gold leaves with the natural red of vine leaves, which look particularly attractive sandwiched between a background of soft green glass and a top layer of clear glass.

1 Draw the pattern on to paper. As it is impossible to see through opal glass, a good way to cut straight lines without marking the glass with a pen is to extend the vertical lines from the square drawn on paper. Place the glass over the pattern so you can see these extensions. Place the cutting square on the glass parallel to these lines. Hold the cutting square firmly and, with the other hand and starting from the top, press and pull the glass cutter towards you. Repeat with the other vertical line to make a strip. Place the glass strip across the square and cut the vertical lines again to make a square. Cut four pale green, four dark green and eight plain glass squares.

YOU WILL NEED

Pattern (see page 72)
Large sheet of white paper
Pen
Cutting square
Opalescent pale green and dark green glass, 30 x 30 cm (12 x 12 in) of each colour
Glass cutter
Grozing pliers
Carborundum stone
2 mm (⅛ in) plain glass, approximately 40 x 40 cm (15 x 15 in)
Clear household glue
Dried leaves, some gold and some plain
8 mm (⁵⁄₁₆ in) copper foil
Wooden or plastic fid
Flux and a brush
Solder and soldering iron
Rubber gloves and sponges
Copper sulphate (copper bright) patina
2 mm (⅛ in) mirror, approximately 15 x 15 cm (6 x 6 in)
Picture wire and snippers

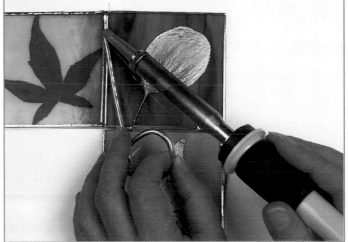

2 Gently file down and wash and dry each piece of glass. Add a tiny drop of glue to the back of a leaf and place it on a square of opalescent glass. Cover with a piece of clear glass and squeeze together. Apply copper foil carefully around the edge of the 'sandwich' with equal amounts protruding on each side. Work around the square and then neatly fold and press the foil on to the sides. Rub down the edges and sides of the foil firmly and smooth out any crinkles with a fid. Repeat this procedure with all the squares of glass.

3 Place the foiled pieces on the pattern, tack into place with flux and solder and then add more flux along the seams. Solder a neat 'bead' of solder where the pieces of glass join. Tin solder the surface edges and turn the frame over. Tin solder the back, then lift the frame on to its edge and solder the inside and outside edges. Very carefully wash with a soapy sponge to remove the flux, then wipe with a damp sponge. Wearing rubber gloves, use a sponge to apply the copper bright patina to the silver solder. When the solder has changed colour, carefully wipe with a dampened soapy sponge and then a rinsed one.

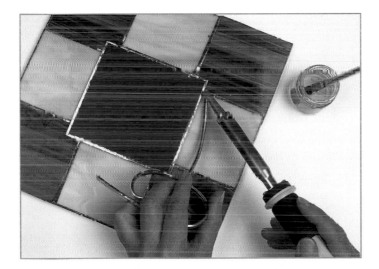

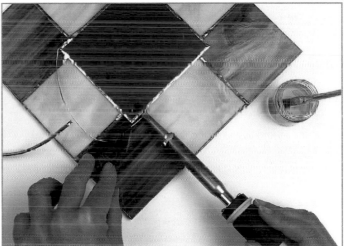

4 Cut a piece of mirror at least 2.5 cm (1 in) longer and wider than the aperture of the centre of the frame. Foil and tin solder. Wash and dry as above. Lay this on the back of the frame, mirror side down. Add a drop of flux where the mirror edge meets a seam of the frame underneath and solder together. Repeat around the other sides.

5 Cut a piece of picture wire with the snippers and, working on the back of the frame, lay one end down the side of the mirror. Flux and solder in position – you may need the pliers to hold and steady the wire as it can become very hot. Leave enough wire to hang the mirror, then secure the other end on the other side of the mirror in the same way. Carefully sponge clean to wipe off residue flux.

TIP

Try not to allow water to seep in-between the pieces of glass when you come to the last stage of washing. However, if a little does find its way don't be too alarmed as it will evaporate.

ETCHED TUMBLERS

You can decorate many household objects to create a frosted or etched look similar to the effect achieved with sandblasting. You can use plain glass, coloured or tinted glass. Areas to be left plain are masked off using a resist such as self-adhesive vinyl. It is a good idea to begin with simple shapes and you can experiment with different types of resists, such as wood glue. For this tumbler I used ordinary kitchen scissors to cut the resist first, but you could apply the resist directly to the vessel and then cut shapes from it using a scalpel or craft knife.

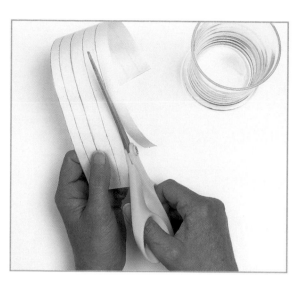

1 On the vinyl, measure three strips 1 cm (½ in) wide and one strip 9 mm (⅜ in) wide. The strips must be long enough to wrap around the glass and to overlap slightly. Cut out the strips with scissors or lay them on a wooden board or plastic cutting mat and slice with a ruler and craft knife.

YOU WILL NEED

Self-adhesive, heavy duty vinyl
to act as the resist

Ruler and pencil

Scissors or scalpel, craft knife and
cutting mat

Glass tumblers

Felt-tipped pen

Plastic bowl

Rubber gloves

Etching paste

Small brush

VARIATIONS

Oil vessels, perfume bottles, jars, flower vases, glass bowls and platters can all be either completely frosted or, with the aid of some simple tools, decorated with designs and motifs in a variety of styles.

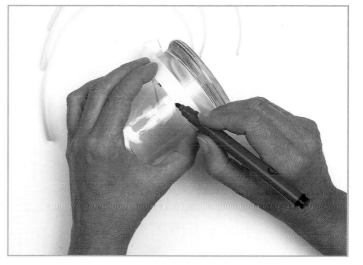

2 Wash and dry the glass tumbler thoroughly. Apply one of the wider strips just above the base of the glass. Pull off the adhesive backing as you go around the glass, pressing the vinyl down firmly with your fingers. Overlap carefully and snip off any extra.

3 Using the paper backing removed from the first strip as a guide, place it next to the first strip of resist. Hold in place and make a tiny mark with the felt-tip pen to indicate where the next piece of resist will be placed. Make several marks around the glass in this way, then apply the next three strips in the same way.

4 Use the narrowest strip of vinyl at the top of the glass. If there is a curve on the surface of the glass, to help the vinyl adhere smoothly without puckering, make some snips in the resist, overlap them and press the resist down well. This is important as the paste must not seep underneath the resist.

5 To apply the paste, wear rubber gloves and work over a plastic bowl. Hold the glass in one hand and paint the paste on to the glass. Keep turning the glass to coat the surface. Consult the instructions for the length of time the paste must remain on the glass. Always read the manufacturer's notes on safety and precautions. Wash off the paste under running water, remove the stencil or resist and allow to dry. Wash again thoroughly before use.

ETCHED GALLERY

Perfume bottle
A simple oil bottle etched with paste and decorated with gold relief outliner.

Glass vase
Wood glue applied in a spiral design provided the resist before the vase was etched.

Shot glasses
Liqueur glasses can be masked with adhesive or resist and etched with paste.

Chequered candle glass
A resist was applied to the glass and the checks cut freehand with a craft knife.

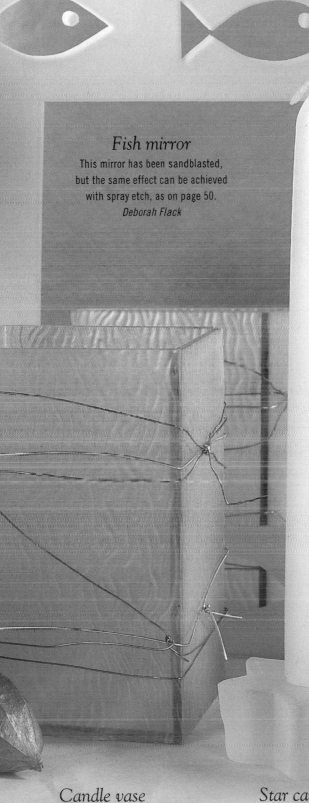

Fish mirror

This mirror has been sandblasted, but the same effect can be achieved with spray etch, as on page 50.
Deborah Flack

Candle vase

Pale yellow cathedral glass has been spray-etched and assembled in the same way as the project on page 26.

Star candle holders

These purchased clear glass holders have been dipped in acid etch paste for a frosted effect.

Candle container

Clear cathedral glass has been frosted with spray etch, assembled with U.V. glue and decorated with wire.

AUTUMN LEAVES

During the autumn I find myself picking up the leaves that spread like a red and gold carpet over the pavements and in the parks. The leaf recreated here in glass is from a London plane tree. The design is excellent either for making in one type of glass (as shown here) or for using up offcuts of glass from other projects. The glass in this project is ideal as it comes in a wonderful range of natural-looking colours

1 Draw the leaf shape onto a sheet of paper using a black felt-tipped pen. Place a piece of glass over the first part of the design you wish to cut. If the glass has a flow of colours, move it around until it is in a position you like. If using fragments of glass, make sure each piece you choose is large enough to cover the individual section.

YOU WILL NEED

Sheet of white paper
Black felt-tipped pen
45 cm² (1½ sq ft) streaky cathedral glass
Glass cutter
Pliers
Carborundum stone
6 mm (¼ in) copper foil
Plastic or wooden fid (or a pencil)
Flux and brush
Soldering iron
Solder (2-3 sticks)
Copper or brass wire
Gloves
Copper sulphate patina
Sponge

TIP

If you are using up small pieces of glass, arrange them so that the joins look like additional veins on the leaf.

2 Using the glass cutter, score along the central vein first. Starting just a fraction in from the side of the glass, press the cutter down very firmly and, with a steady hand, follow the line on the pattern beneath. Keep the pressure even and continue scoring until you reach the other side of the glass, just beyond the top of the leaf. Gently tap the glass under the score and break apart. Cut all the other pieces of glass in the same way. You can also use the pliers to help break the glass apart.

3 Place the cut pieces of glass over the pattern and check you are happy with the fit and the way the colours work together. Then rub down the edge of the glass on the carborundum stone to remove sharp slivers. Rinse the glass in water to remove any dust and dry, then wrap each edge in copper foil. Place the edge in the centre of the foil and wrap around, overlapping at the point where you started. Fold the edges of the foil over the sides and rub gently with a fid or pencil.

4 Brush on the flux and tack solder the pieces so they stay in place, then flux and solder the seams. Apply just enough solder to form a bead covering the joints. Move the iron slowly along the seam, melting the solder as you go. Remember to apply flux before soldering a new seam. Only apply a thin coat to 'tin' the surface edges of the leaf while the piece lies flat.

5 When the seams have been soldered on both sides, lift the leaf and flux the outer edges. Apply just enough solder to coat the edges — too much will dribble off the foil and onto the glass. If you discover lumps have formed when soldering the seams, melt these along the foil with the soldering iron and smooth them out.

6 Cut a length of brass wire (the length will depend on where you wish to hang the leaf). Fold the wire in half and twist it together, leaving a small loop at the top. Lay the wire down the central seam on the back and brush with flux. Melt enough solder to cover the wire and secure it to the seam below. Wash the finished leaf in warm, soapy water then, wearing gloves, apply copper sulphate patina with a sponge and wash once more.

MIRROR BROOCH

Glass nuggets are some of the most useful and eye-catching glass accessories. They can be copper-foiled and incorporated into windows and lampshades. Available in a variety of sizes and colours, they are inexpensive and are often used in jewellery projects. Placed on the reflective background of mirror glass they resemble large jewels. Offcuts of glass left over from larger projects often have appealing shapes. Look out for these shapes as you work on projects – you may have some small and attractive pieces just waiting to be made into a piece of jewellery.

1 Look for small scraps of mirrored glass that may be suitable or alternatively draw your own shape with a felt-tipped pen onto the reflective surface of a piece of mirror. Score the shape and break apart.

YOU WILL NEED

Offcuts of 2 mm (⅛ in) mirror
Felt-tipped pen
Glass cutter
Grozing pliers
Carborundum stone
5 mm (⁷⁄₃₂ in) silver-backed copper foil
Wooden or plastic fid
Flux and brush
Solder (lead-free is available if you prefer)
Soldering iron
Clear household glue or optical glue
One medium and one small clear nugget, one small pale blue nugget
Jewellery pliers
Silver-plated wire
Pin fastening (available from bead and jewellery suppliers)

TIP

The soldering iron shown here has a special jewellery tip which is available from stained glass suppliers.

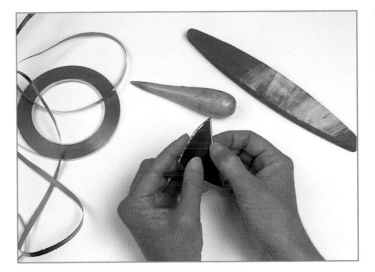

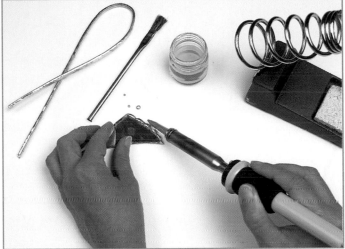

2 Gently rub the edges onto a carborundum stone, especially any pointed pieces. Rinse in water to remove any glass dust and dry thoroughly. Apply copper foil to the edge of the piece. Fold the foil over the sides, making sure the foil is even all around. Flatten the sides down and rub out any crinkles with a fid.

3 Apply some flux over the copper foil and tin solder the front, back and sides. Then gather a little extra solder on the tip of the iron. Very carefully touch the edges with the tip of the iron and allow tiny decorative bumps to form. Add a little more flux as you work around the edge, continuing to form a series of bumps. Wash the piece well in soapy warm water with a sponge and dry. Apply a small amount of clear adhesive to the back of the nuggets and arrange them on the mirror surface. Leave to set.

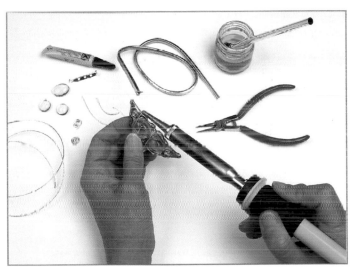

4 To make the silver decorations, grasp the end of the silver wire with the jewellery pliers. Make a tight inward twist and, at the same time, move the other end of the wire underneath, keeping the silver wire close to the next curl. Continue to curl and bend and then snip off.

5 Wrap a length of silver wire around the brooch and over and around the glass pebbles. Snip off the wire and press down against the edges. Add a tiny touch of flux and a very small amount of solder to secure the wire to the side. Place the spirals onto the brooch and secure in the same way. Gently wash in warm soapy water and dry, then use some adhesive to attach the brooch pin to the back.

WARNING

The silver wire can become hot so use pliers to hold
the piece if necessary.

Flower mirror
Pressed flowers have been
sandwiched between two
pieces of clear glass and
copper foiled, similar to
the project on page 30.
Janet Crook

Wire-edged frames
Small pieces of glass have been
copper foiled, soldered and
embellished with copper wire.
Janet Crook

Butterfly

Streaky cathedral glass in various colours is used in this mobile.

Hanging leaves

These decorative hangings for a window are made in the same way as the project on page 36.

Crimson picture frame

This is made in the same way as the project on page 54, but with a black patina finish.

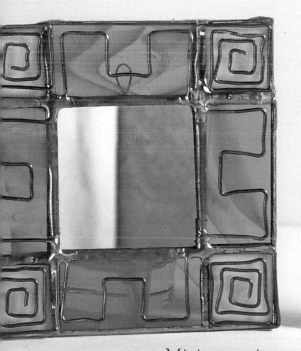

Miniature mirror

A pretty mirror made with copper foil and decorated with wire. *Janet Crook*

GLASS PENDANT

The inspiration for this jewellery came from small offcuts left from other projects. The blue is a small piece of cathedral glass I had already sprayed with glass etch. It is simply placed etched side down on the reflective side of a piece of mirror glass of the same size. Lead-free solder is available from stained glass suppliers. You may prefer to use this when making jewellery. Placing pressed flowers between two pieces of glass also makes very attractive jewellery.

1 Cut a piece of mirror and a piece of coloured glass the same size. Rub gently on a carborundum stone to remove any sharp edges, then wash and dry. If using etched glass, place this etched side down on the reflective side of the mirror. Foil the edges, ensuring there is a small amount of foil on either side of the glass to fold onto the surface.

YOU WILL NEED

Glass and mirror offcuts
Glass cutter
Grozing pliers
Carborundum stone
5 mm (⁷⁄₃₂ in) or 6 mm (¼ in) silver-backed copper foil
Plastic or wooden fid
Flux and brush
Solder
Soldering iron
Jewellery pliers
Silver-plated wire
Silver jump rings (available from bead and jewellery suppliers)
Black leather thong or silver chain

TIP

The soldering iron shown in this project has a special jewellery tip which is available from stained glass suppliers.

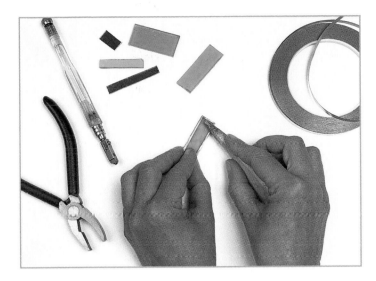

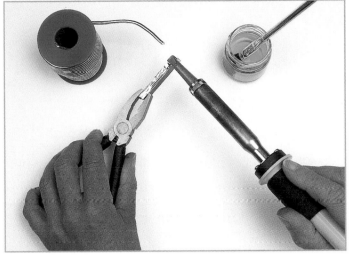

2 On a small piece of jewellery such as this, you need to make sure the foiling is neat – you can wrap the foil around the glass a second time if necessary. Rub the foil down very carefully along the sides and the edges of the glass with a fid until it is smooth.

3 As the piece is so small, when soldering, use the pliers or long tweezers to hold the piece as it can become very hot. Apply some flux over the copper foil and then solder the sides and edges, ensuring the finish is smooth. Clean thoroughly with a soapy sponge and rinse.

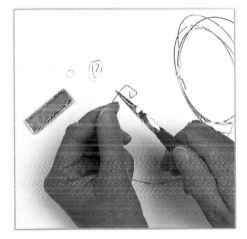

4 To make the silver decoration, hold the jewellery pliers approximately 1 cm (½ in) from the end of the wire, and bend the wire sharply. Make a few more bends in a similar way until you have a pleasing shape. Snip off the coil. You can adjust the shape with your fingers.

5 Place the silver coil on the glass and melt a tiny drop of solder onto the side or end of the coil where it touches the soldered edges of the glass. You may need just a dab of flux. Repeat with the second coil.

6 Grasp a jump ring firmly with the pliers and hold it against the top of the glass, add a touch of flux and then melt a tiny amount of solder on to the jump ring and attach to the edge of the glass. Sponge clean once again, and thread a thong or chain through the jump ring.

LIGHTCATCHER

Creating something from glass to hang in a window can be as absorbing and challenging as making a panel to fit a specific site. When caught by the sunshine, the glass can cast the most beautiful effects within a room. If the glass object has some freedom of movement as well, the reflected light has the qualities of a watercolour effect. The wire used to create the basic shape is called welding rod. If you have trouble finding it, try your local garage.

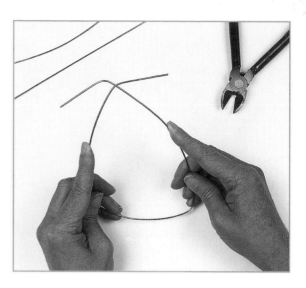

1 Use the snips to cut the welding rod to length and shape it following the pattern. Bend the ends towards each other and then cross them over. The idea is to take the tension out of the wire. When you have bent the wire sufficiently for the two ends to stay closed or sit as near as possible, it is ready to be soldered together.

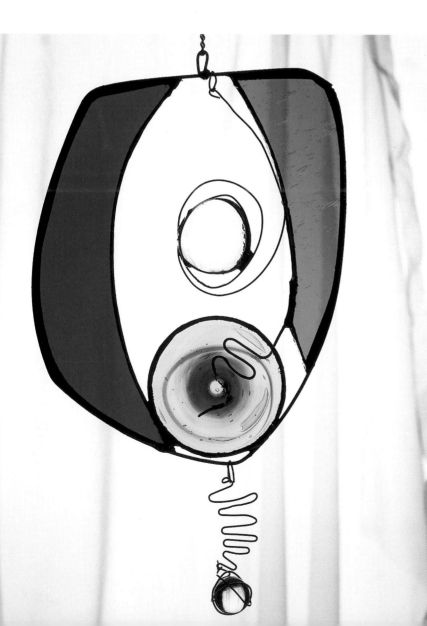

YOU WILL NEED

Cutting snips
50 cm (20 in) length of welding rod, heavy gauge brass wire or copper wire
Pattern (see page 74)
Flux and brush
Solder
Soldering iron
Sheet of paper and a pen
Red or yellow roundel
Dark blue semi-antique glass, 30 x 15 cm (12 x 6 in)
Pale blue semi-antique glass, 30 x 15 cm (12 x 6 in)
Glass cutter
Grozing pliers
Carborundum stone
5 mm (⁷/₃₂ in) silver-backed copper foil
Plastic or wooden fid
15 cm (6 in) length of copper wire
Large, flat, clear glass nugget
Silver-plated wire
Jewellery pliers
Glass ball
Nylon thread, fishing wire or chain for hanging

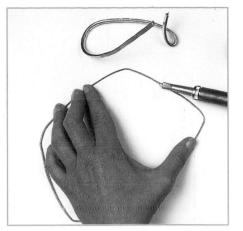

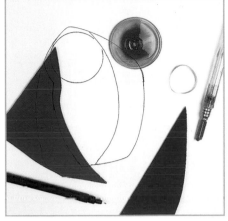

2 Lay the wire flat and hold it so that the two ends meet. Add some flux and keep the solder near you. Touch the solder with the iron to gather some on the tip of the iron. Melt this onto the two ends of the wire or rod. Hold the wire together for about 15 seconds to make sure the ends have joined. When the wire is soldered and secure, you can adjust the shape to fit the outline of the pattern. You can also create your own pattern with the shape you have made with the wire.

3 Once bent into a shape you like, lay the wire onto the paper and draw around the inside as a pattern. Place the roundel inside the shape and draw around it. Now draw some free-hand shapes for the dark and pale blue glass within this outline. Lay the glass over this pattern and score and cut out these pieces of glass.

4 File and foil the two pieces of blue glass plus the roundel. Flux and tin solder these pieces to the wire form. Turn over and tin the back of the pieces as well.

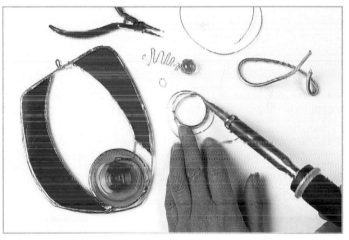

5 Bend the end of a small piece of copper wire into an attractive shape and lay it across the back of the roundel. Solder one end along the soldered edge of the pale blue glass. Create a small loop with a piece of copper wire and attach it with solder to the top of the panel. Gently wash the lightcatcher in warm soapy water to remove the flux.

6 File the edges of the large nugget and wash and copper foil it. Solder the end of some silver-plated wire to the foil and wind it loosely around the nugget, continuing to attach with solder at various points. Gently wash and dry the nugget/silver ornament. Make a small loop of wire and attach it to the top of the lightcatcher. Twist the end of the silver wire into a hook and hang it off the loop so it swings freely within the centre of the lightcatcher. Wrap a glass ball in silver-plated wire and create another twisted hanging decoration for the bottom. Tie a length of thread or chain to the loop at the top of the panel and hang in a window.

─────── TIP ───────

Silver-plated wire is available from jewellery suppliers.

LEADED LIGHT

This small window has been made with lead, a centuries' old method of assembling stained glass windows. It includes some bevels – cut pieces of glass with polished faceted edges – which you can buy in a variety of shapes and sizes. Combining different types of glass within a window can create a pretty effect. Here, I have also used water glass and machine-made glass with a rippled surface texture. Always make at least two or even three identical copies of the pattern – one for cutting and one to pin to a wooden board to lead the piece together.

YOU WILL NEED

Pattern (see page 75)	Lead vice (optional)
Medium-sized felt-tipped pen	Lead knife
Piece of wood, approximately 30 x 37.5 cm (12 x 15 in)	12 horseshoe nails
	Four 5 cm (2 in) bevels
Two wooden battens, 2.5 x 4 cm (1 x 1½ in), long enough to fit around two sides of the board	One 12.5 cm (5 in) diamond-shaped bevel
	Wooden or plastic fid
Hammer	Tallow candle
Nails	Wire brush (optional)
30 x 30 cm (12 x 12 in) turquoise water glass	Soldering iron
	Solder
30 x 30 cm (12 x 12 in) pale yellow rippled cathedral glass	Lead light cement and brush
	Protective gloves
Glass cutter	Whiting
9 mm (⅜ in) lead came	Fire grate blackener
6 mm (¼ in) lead came	

1 Draw the design onto paper with a felt-tipped pen. The lines should be approximately 2 mm (1/16 in) wide (they represent the heart of the lead). Check the heart of the narrower lead as a guide. When cutting the glass allow for a gap the width of this heart in-between each piece. Draw a pencil line around the perimeter of the design half the width of the wider outside lead. Lay the pattern on the flat piece of wood and nail down the battens at right angles next to these pencil lines. Using the other pattern, cut all the pieces of glass in preparation for leading.

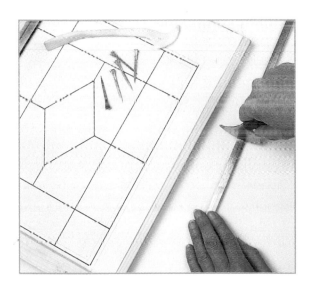

2 The lead should be stretched before you use it to straighten out any bends. Clamp it into a lead vice which has been fixed to a table, or get someone to pull one end of the lead while you hold the other end with pliers. To cut the lead, place the knife on top of the came and press down, moving the knife gently but firmly from side to side (left to right).

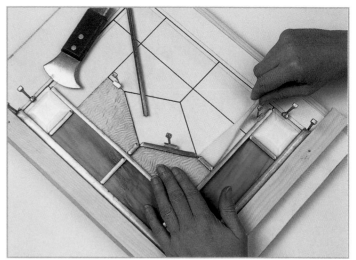

3 Cut two strips of the wider lead, one the length of the pattern and one the width of the pattern. Place at right angles within the battens. Hold them in place with a horseshoe nail at each end, tapped into the wood with the end of the knife. Place the cut pieces of glass into the open channel of lead. If it has closed, open it slightly by running the fid along the channel.

Cut short lengths of the narrower lead came and place them between each section of glass. Remember to make an allowance for the adjacent piece of lead. You can measure and make a small mark with the knife on the lead first, then place it on a flat surface before cutting through with the knife.

4 Place more pieces of glass into the channels of lead and cut and lay another piece of lead to slot onto the glass. Use the fid to push the lead gently against the glass. You will have to cut angles from the lead to accommodate the central bevel. Continue placing the glass and lead. Finally, cut two more outside pieces of wider lead and lay within the outside pencil lines. Hold all the glass in place as you work with horseshoe nails, with a small piece of lead in-between to protect the edge of the glass.

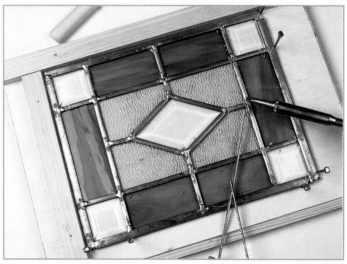

5 When the panel is complete, rub on tallow candle at the joints. If the lead is a little oxidized you can rub the joints first with a wire brush. There will inevitably be some gaps where one piece of lead has not quite met the next. As long as they are only tiny these can be filled with little slivers of lead sliced from leftover scraps.

6 Switch on the iron and when it is ready apply only enough solder to cover the junctions where the lead cames meet. Be very careful as the iron can melt the lead beneath if you leave it on for more than a few seconds. Melt a small amount of solder onto the tip of the iron and place it onto the lead. Count to three and lift the iron off.

TIP

The lead comes in long strips of milled cames and has a central 'heart'. When cutting the glass you must make an allowance for this.

7 When you have completed the soldering on both sides, the panel is ready for cementing. This form of putty makes the panel strong and weather-proof. Scoop out some of the cement from the pot with a fid and lay it onto the panel. Wearing protective gloves and using a brush, start to push the cement around and work it under the lead cames. The idea is to fill all the gaps between the glass and the cames.

When you have finished one side, scatter some whiting powder over the panel and rub around with your gloved hand. This will absorb the oil from the cement. Turn the panel over and repeat on the other side. You can wait for half an hour before turning the panel over or do both and then wait for the cement to start to dry before proceeding with the next step.

8 Depending on the temperature of the room, the cement will start to dry fairly quickly. After about half an hour start to draw the fid around the cames to release and remove the excess cement. The other end of the fid is useful for lifting off any excess on the glass itself.

9 Once much of the excess cement is removed, start to brush the panel. Brush quite vigorously across the cames and the glass. It will loosen and remove all the unwanted bits of cement and clean both the lead and the glass. Turn the panel over and repeat on the other side. You can still use the pointed end of the fid to tidy and clean the sides of the lead as before.

10 Give the lead a final rubbing with a clean brush. You can add a tiny amount of fire grate blackener to the brush and continue the brushing. The more you brush, the darker the cames will become. This panel can be framed in wood or fitted into an existing window. You can also easily adapt the pattern to the size you require.

ETCHED MIRROR

Etching the surface of plain or coloured glass is usually achieved with the aid of a sandblasting machine. However, with the use of acid paste or spray etch, similar decorative effects can be easily made without the need to find a sandblasting facility. You can create a frosted effect on mirror as well as vessels such as vases or other objects. Spray etch works particularly well on mirror glass and can give a striking effect very quickly. Remember to read the manufacturer's instructions carefully before use.

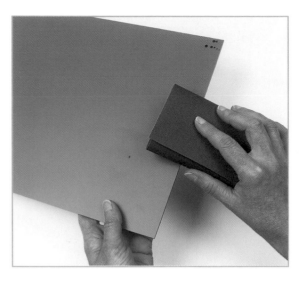

1 Lay the cutting square on the reflective surface of the mirror and using felt-tipped pen, draw a rectangle 30 x 25 cm (12 x 10 in). Cut out the rectangle in the same way as cutting glass. Dip the sandpaper in some water and wrap it around a block of wood. Gently rub along the edges of the mirror glass and make sure all edges are polished and smooth. Clean the mirror thoroughly.

YOU WILL NEED

Mirror glass, at least 30 x 25 cm (12 x 10 in)
Fine felt-tipped pen
Cutting square
Glass cutter
Grozing pliers
Wet and dry sandpaper
Small square of wood
Resist paper, slightly larger than the mirror
Scalpel or craft knife
Ruler and fine pen
Spray etch
Brass key mount with screws
Small block of wood, no thicker than 2.5 cm (1 in)
Pieces of coloured glass in random shapes
Optical glue (ultraviolet)

TIP
Several light coats of spray etch give a better result than one heavy one.

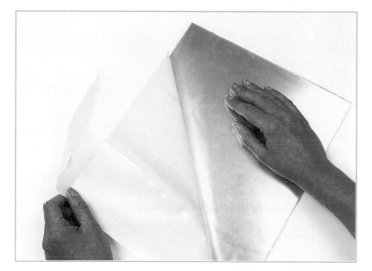

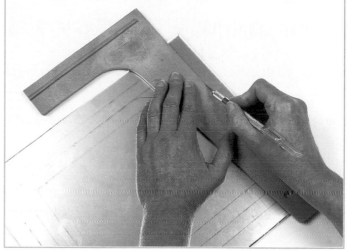

2 Cut a piece of resist paper the same size or slightly larger than the mirror. Peel back the first 2.5 cm (1 in) of the protective paper from the resist and lay the adhesive side onto the mirror. Smooth the resist onto the surface. Continue to peel off the paper backing, smoothing down the resist as you work.

3 Measure in 5 cm (2 in) from the sides, top and bottom edges of the mirror. Make marks with a fine felt-tipped pen. Following these marks, draw a rectangle in the centre. Divide the border into three and mark again with a pen. Join all the marks so you have three parallel bands around the border. Lay the cutting square next to the pen lines and use the scalpel to cut through the resist.

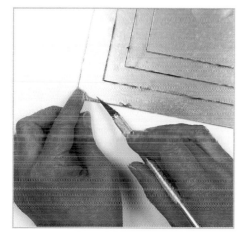

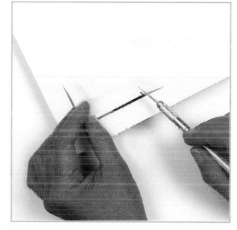

4 Pick up the outsides edge of the resist and gently peel off the outer border first. Make sure the middle border does not lift off as well. Take off the inner border resist in the same way. Rub down the remaining middle border and central rectangle of resist if the edges have been disturbed. Following the manufacturer's instructions on the can, spray the etch in an even sweep, moving from left to right down the mirror. Apply one light coat. Allow five minutes for it to dry, then spray one or two more coats.

5 After about one hour the spray etch on the mirror should be touch dry (check the manufacturer's instructions for precise drying times). Carefully peel off the remaining resist. You may need a craft knife to lift the resist paper.

6 Screw the brass key mount onto the block of wood. Apply some adhesive to the other side of the wood and fix to the back of the mirror. Leave to dry. Glue some shapes of coloured glass to the front of the mirror.

HANGING ROUNDEL

Traditional painting on stained glass involves working with oxide paints and firing the painted glass in a kiln. However, there are paints available that can be applied to glass for an instant effect. These are especially useful for decorating small objects.

They simply have to be allowed to dry and there is no kiln work involved, making them ideal for use at home. Within the range is a black 'contour' paste, or outliner, which simulates lead lines. In this mobile the outliner highlights the colours of the glass beneath.

1 Lay a piece of glass over the shapes of the pattern and score with the cutter. Hold the piece of glass firmly in one hand while placing the pliers near the score with the other. Grip and snap apart.

YOU WILL NEED

Scraps of pale blue, orange and lilac semi-antique glass, or approximately 7.5 x 7.5 cm (3 x 3 in) of each

Pattern (see page 74)

Glass cutter

Grozing pliers

1 pale blue roundel

Carborundum stone

5 mm (7/32 in) copper foil (silver backed)

Wooden or plastic fid

Flux and a brush

Solder

Soldering iron

Jump rings – 3 large and 7 small (available from jewellery suppliers)

Jewellery pliers (or tweezers)

Tube of black contour paste (or outliner)

Strong thread or fishing thread

VARIATIONS

These paints can also be used to create decorative effects on other glass objects such as vases and bottles.

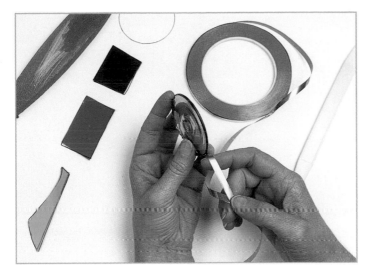

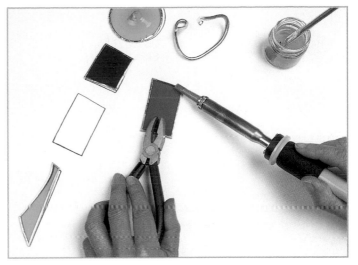

2 Rub the edges of the roundel on the carborundum stone, wash and dry, and then foil. Place the edge of the roundel in the centre of the foil and press the foil on to the glass. Continue around the circle, overlap and cut the foil. Fold down the foil onto the sides of the roundel and smooth down carefully with a fid. File and foil all the pieces in the same way.

3 Apply flux to the piece and tin solder the edges of the foiled pieces of glass and roundel. It will be necessary to hold the pieces of glass with the pliers while tin soldering as such small pieces become hot during the process.

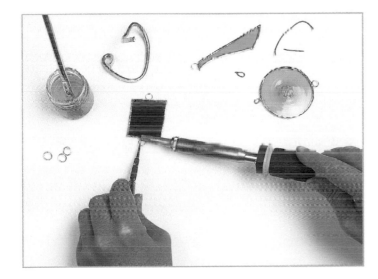

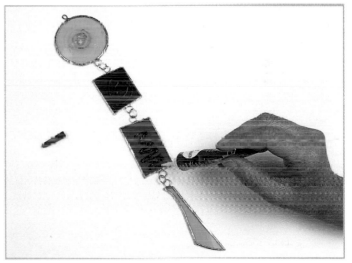

4 Add the small jump rings to the top and bottom of the pieces of glass. Hold the ring with jewellery pliers and place it against the side of the glass. Add just enough solder to attach the ring to the soldered edge of the glass. Wash each piece carefully in warm soapy water. Allow to dry. Now open the large jump rings and loop them through the rings attached to the glass. Close carefully with the pliers.

5 Practise using the contour paste on some paper or scraps of glass. Squeeze the tube and create a spiral or decorative squiggle. Apply it to the pieces of the mobile while they lie flat on the table. Allow the paint or paste to dry before you hang it with strong thread or fishing thread.

PICTURE FRAME

Elaborate picture frames can sometimes detract from the photograph you want to display. This coloured glass frame is effectively simple and enhances an image placed within. You could make it in a choice of colours, choosing a complementary shade to co-ordinate with a particular photograph or image. It would also make a lovely gift, with a photo of the recipient already inserted. Made in a bright, transparent colour, the light can penetrate through the front of the frame, casting a reflected colour onto the surface behind.

1 Lay the glass over the pattern and, using the cutter, accurately score the glass following the lines beneath. Remember to press down quite hard. Either tap underneath the score lines or break apart using the grozing pliers. Use pieces of glass that are not too much bigger than the shape you want but allow for a good 'margin' of glass around each shape to be cut. Cut the five outer pieces in green plus the central shape in clear plain glass. Rub the cut edges with a carborundum stone.

YOU WILL NEED

Transparent antique or semi-antique glass, 15 x 15 cm (6 x 6 in)
2 mm (⅛ in) clear glass (picture glass), 7.5 x 7.5 cm (3 x 3 in)
Pattern (see page 76)
Glass cutter
Grozing pliers
Carborundum stone
4 mm (³⁄₁₆ in) silver-backed copper foil
Plastic or wooden fid
Flux and brush
Solder
Soldering iron
Approximately 43 cm (17 in) galvanized steel wire
15 cm (6 in) copper wire
Photograph and piece of backing card

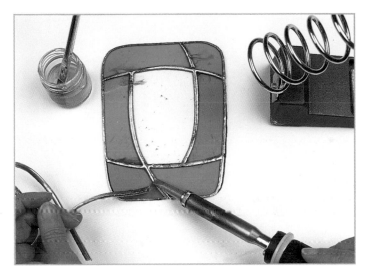

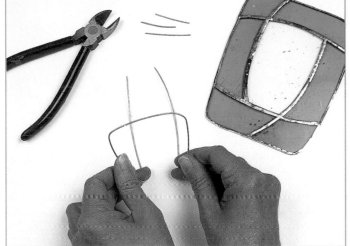

2 Wrap all the pieces of glass in copper foil and rub down with a fid. Brush with flux and tack solder to hold in place. Do this by melting a little solder with the iron to form a blob on these areas. Then continue to apply flux to the rest of the frame. Bead solder the front of the frame and tin solder the sides and back.

3 To make the back support for the frame, hold the two ends of the galvanized wire together and place on a surface with your fingers resting about 10 cm (4 in) from the ends. Press with your fingers down on to the surface to bend the wire and push the loop that is left backwards with your thumbs.

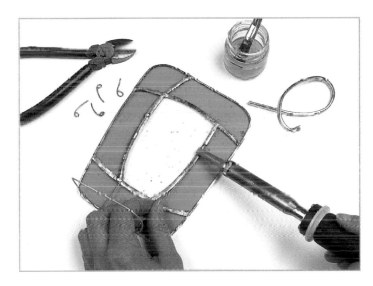

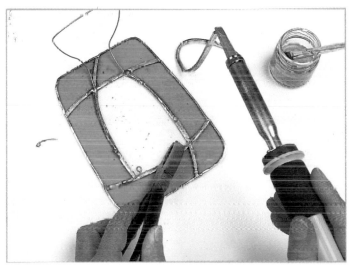

4 Lay the picture frame face down on the work surface and hold one end of the wire along the seam between the frame and the clear glass. Apply some flux and then melt a blob of solder to secure the end of the wire. Use pliers to hold the wire in place and flux and solder the remaining length. Secure the other end in the same way on the other side of the frame. The wire can now be manipulated if necessary into a suitable shape and angle to support the frame and rest steadily on a surface.

5 Using the pliers or snippers, curl an end of the copper wire and then snip off a length of about 2 cm (¾ in). Make three more curls in the same way. Solder on these pieces of wire using pliers to hold in place. These will be used to hold a photo plus protective backing in place over the clear glass. Wash and dry the frame. Cut a photo and a piece of backing card to the shape of the central clear panel. Lift up the copper tags, place the photo on the glass with card and then gently press down the tags to hold secure.

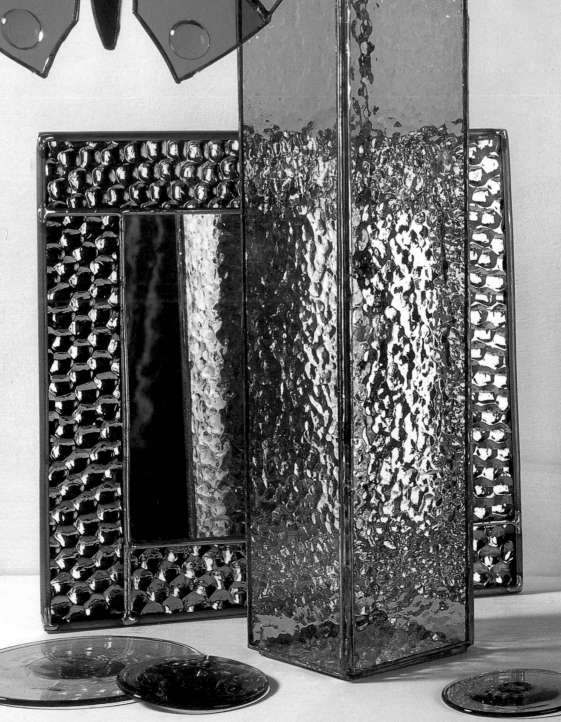

Picture frame
(facing page)
This is made in water glass with a clear glass centre. A hanging wire is soldered to the back.

Golden vase
This tall vase is made with cathedral glass and assembled with copper foil.

Butterfly mobile
Glass nuggets are attached to the glass with U.V. glue. The decorative copper wire is soldered to the seams.

Yellow mirror
This attractive mirror is made with copper foil and edged with lead.
Anji Marfleet

Wire-edged mirror
This mirror is copper foiled and tinned, with copper wire spirals soldered to the edges.
Janet Crook

Faceted box
Made with opalescent glass and copper foil, the lid of this box simply rests on the top.

THREE-DIMENSIONAL STAR

This simple star is a good example of how suited copper foil is to three-dimensional projects. The bottom cone of the star is elongated, creating an elegant overall shape. When soldering the cones together, you may need some sort of support, such as pens or pencils, to hold the cones in the correct positions.

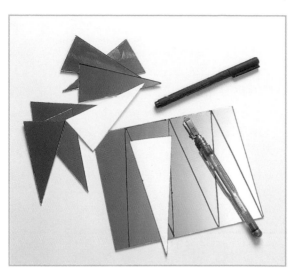

1 Place the patterns on the reflective surface of the glass and draw around them with the felt-tipped pen. You will need four large triangles and 20 smaller triangles. You can draw the triangles side by side on the glass and cut strips of glass first, then score the sides to make the individual triangles.

YOU WILL NEED

Patterns (see page 76)
Fine felt-tipped pen
2 mm mirror glass, 60 x 30 cm (24 x 12 in)
Cutting square
Glass cutter
Grozing pliers
Carborundum stone
5 or 6 mm (⁷⁄₃₂ or ¼ in) copper foil
Flux and brush
Solder
Soldering iron
Pens or pencils (to act as props)
A length of copper wire (for the hanging loop)

VARIATIONS

For a different effect, this star could be made in coloured glass —
either in one colour or a selection of shades.

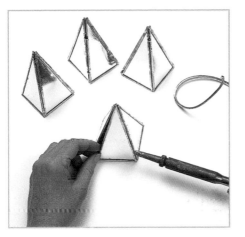

2 Using the cutting square to ensure the lines are straight, score the triangles and snap apart. You may need to use the pliers to help snap the narrow end. Rub all the sides of the triangles gently with the carborundum stone.

3 Wash each piece of glass to remove any glass dust and then dry. Copper foil all the sides of the triangles. Flux and tin solder each piece of glass separately, then wash again in warm soapy water and dry.

4 Assemble four of the smaller triangles into a cone and tack solder together. Repeat with the remaining triangles to make another four small cones and one large cone.

5 Once the triangles are held in position, hold one of the cones on its side and carefully run more solder down all the seams. Repeat with the remaining cones.

6 Place two of the small cones at right angles, propping them up on pencils or pens so that the top edges are horizontal. Flux and solder together. Add the larger cone and solder in position, then add a third small cone to complete the square opening in the centre of the star.

7 Flux and solder another small cone in position, on top of the square opening. Turn the star over and solder the final cone in position. Neaten the soldering along all the seams. Solder a small brass loop to the top of the star (to the top of the small cone opposite the large cone). If the star is awkward to hold, rest it inside a small box. Wash the star in warm soapy water and dry.

AEGEAN CANDLE BOX

As opalescent glass is opaque, unless you have a
light box you are unable to see through it when
it is laid on to a pattern. For this reason, make
an extra copy of the pattern and cut out the
shapes that will be made from white opalescent
glass. Lay these pieces of paper on top of the
white glass and mark around them with a fine
felt-tipped pen. You can then cut the shapes out
of the glass following these lines.

This candle box has two patterns for the sides,
marked A and B. Make up two sides of pattern
A and two of pattern B as four separate pieces
before assembling them into the shape of a
square box. A and B are placed alternately.

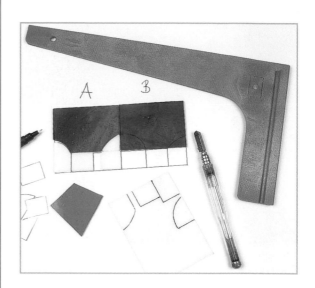

1 Place pattern A and B together and cut out
the blue glass using the cutting square,
checking that the pieces match the adjacent
pattern. After scoring and breaking the straight
lines, lay the glass back on the pattern and score
the curves, following the lines of the pattern. Lay
the shapes cut from a spare pattern on the white
glass and outline with a felt-tipped pen. Score and
break the white shapes, plus the turquoise ones.

YOU WILL NEED

Three copies of the pattern (see page 76)
30 x 30 cm (12 x 12 in) blue streaky cathedral glass
Glass cutter
Cutting square
Grozing pliers
30 x 30 cm (12 x 12 in) white opalescent glass
Fine felt-tipped pen
7.5 x 7.5 cm (3 x 3 in) turquoise semi-antique glass
Carborundum stone
5 mm ($\frac{1}{32}$ in) copper foil
7.5 x 7.5 cm (3 x 3 in) mirror glass
Flux and a brush
Solder
Soldering iron
Rubber gloves
Copper bright patina
Sponge
4 small flat white marbles or glass nuggets
Household glue

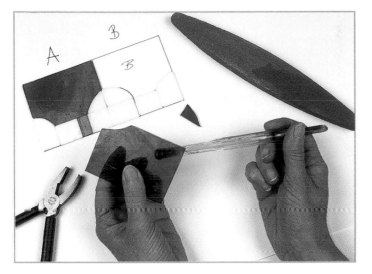

2 Tap the curve with the ball end of the cutter underneath the score. When tapping out a curve you may be left with sharp slivers of glass along the edges. Use the grozing pliers or file to remove these slivers prior to foiling. File all the pieces of glass, wash and dry, and then wrap with the foil. Cut and foil a piece of mirrored glass for the bottom of the box in the same way.

3 Solder each of the four sides individually. Arrange onto the pattern and flux and tack solder to hold them in place before bead soldering the front and tinning the back and sides. Flux and tin solder the piece of mirrored glass.

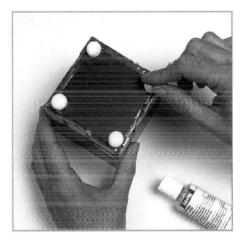

4 Place two sides together (one A and one B), butting the edges up to each other. You may need to use a glass tumbler or something similar to support the pieces while you add a drop of solder to hold in place. Add the third and fourth pieces in the same way.

5 Turn the box onto its side and solder the seams carefully, adding enough solder to form a smooth bead. When the seams are soldered you can place the box over the square of mirrored glass – it should be a snug fit inside the box. Attach it with a drop of solder and turn the box upside down. Tin solder the seams on the underneath of the box.

6 Wash the box thoroughly in warm soapy water and dry. This will remove any oil from the cutter and flux. Using rubber gloves apply the copper bright patina to the solder. Rub the sponge over these areas until all the silver solder has turned a coppery colour. Wash the box again in warm soapy water and dry. Attach the flat marbles to the corners of the base of the box with glue and leave to set.

--- TIP ---

Copper foil is a very versatile method for holding pieces of glass together, especially three-dimensional objects such as boxes, as its flexibility means you can wrap very small pieces of glass with foil. The narrower the foil you use, the finer the finished seam will become.

TIFFANY WINDOW

This panel was inspired by one of Louis Comfort Tiffany's great windows and is made with copper foil, a method he created. It is important to make an identical copy of the pattern. Use one to cut out the pieces of glass and, as you work, transfer the cut pieces on to the other pattern. Check your work as you go, making sure you have cut each piece to the correct shape.

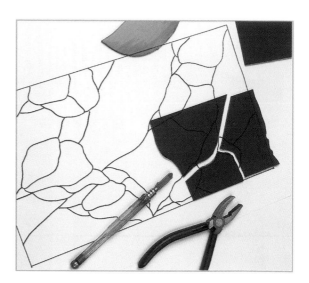

1 Place the glass over the area of pattern you wish to work on and start to score the glass. This pattern has some sharp angles. Instead of struggling to follow such sharp bends with one score, make many, moving off the edge of the glass. Complete all the scores before picking up the glass and tapping underneath with the other end of the cutter.

YOU WILL NEED

Two copies of the pattern
(see page 77)

30 x 30 cm (12 x 12 in)
deep pink rolled cathedral glass

30 x 30 cm (12 x 12 in)
clear antique glass

7.5 x 7.5 cm (3 x 3 in)
green semi-antique glass

Glass cutter

Grozing pliers

Carborundum stone

Flux and a brush

Solder

Soldering iron

5 mm (7/32 in) copper foil

Wooden or plastic fid

TIP

Copper foil is amazingly strong once soldered and is very useful for using with intricate designs and small pieces of glass.

2 When glass has been tapped out, it has a tendency to leave behind sharp slivers of glass hanging on the edges. Remove these pieces with the grozing pliers. Put the glass within the jaws of the pliers and close them loosely. Now drag the pliers down and backwards. Take off the sharp points on the glass as well.

3 Carefully file along the edges of all the pieces of glass with the carborundum stone. It may be necessary to wash these pieces in water to remove the glass dust. Dry the pieces thoroughly before beginning step 4.

4 Place the edges of the glass in the centre of the foil. Press this adhesive side against the glass as you continue to pull back the protective paper and move around the glass. Overlap where you started and cut or break the foil. Fold down the foil onto the sides of the glass and then lay the glass onto the table. Smooth down the foil with a fid.

5 Place all the foiled pieces back on the pattern and check they fit well. Flux and tack solder in place and then flux again and bead solder the front. Always move very slowly with the iron to ensure a smooth finish. You can tidy up seams you are not happy with by re-touching with the hot iron. Always allow the iron to re-heat the solder so it can become near liquid and flow. Bring the iron off the seam slowly.

6 When the front is finished, turn the panel over and tin solder the back. Use just enough solder to coat the foil and cover the joins. Some solder may have seeped through from the front. Use this to help tin the back. Tin solder the side edges of the panel and then wash well with a soapy sponge and rinse in clear water. This panel has not had a patina applied. If you prefer the solder to turn a copper colour, apply copper bright.

WINDOW GALLERY

Palms

Lynette Wrigley
43 x 58 cm (17 x 23 in)
A panel framed to hang in a window. The palms were assembled with copper foil, allowing the use of the smallest pieces of glass to create the overlapping detail and intricacy of the leaves.

Sunflowers

Lynette Wrigley
97 x 81 cm (38 x 32 in)
The spectacular bloom of the sunflower has been captured in antique glass and assembled in lead. The head has been detailed with vitreous paint and fired in a kiln. Made for a window above a front door.

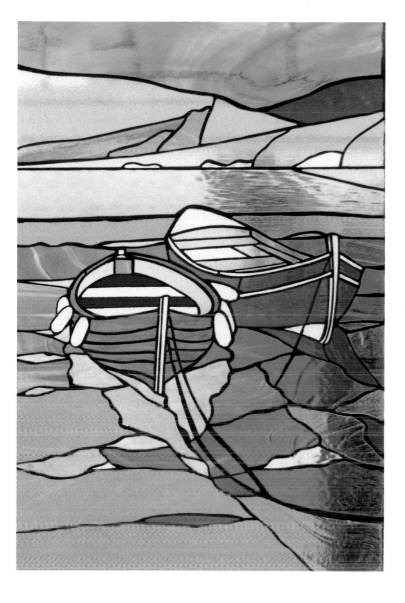

Boats

Lynette Wrigley
91 x 60 cm (36 x 24 in)
A brightly coloured window
for a door leading into a
conservatory. Made with
copper foil, it uses antique
and water glass, enhancing
the reflections of light and
movement of the water.

Kitchen door panel

Lynette Wrigley
30 x 94 cm (12 x 37 in)
One of two door panels made in
antique glass, assembled in
lead and decorated with
painted spirals and a pear. The
upper motif is sandblasted.

River window

Lynette Wrigley
84 x 28 cm (33 x 11 in)
A fanlight window above a front door reflects the movement and colours of the
river beyond. Made with English and Polish antique glass and assembled in
lead. Paint has been used to extend the sweep of the lead lines.

Edwardian flower window

Helen Robinson
84 x 38 cm (33 x 15 in)
This leaded window combines graphic design with powerful colours set against clear textured glass. It was made for a bedroom transom window in an Edwardian house.

Birchwood and bluebells

Helen Robinson
Three panels, each 50 x 50 cm (20 x 20 in)

Made for a woodland home and inspired by both the setting and the design on a quilt, this window uses fractures and streamers glass for the background and opalescent glass with a dappled texture. Assembled in lead and set in triple glazed panels.

Bluebells

Helen Robinson
55 cm (22 in) in diameter
This leaded roundel uses antique glass for a subtly
textured background. The design has an Art Nouveau
feel and is based on Arts and Crafts windows
featuring stylized botanical studies.

The tree of life

Wolfe van Brussel
45 cm (17½ in) in diameter
The animated design and lively colours of this window were
inspired by the Welsh folktale in which a tree, at once both green
and burning, leads to the Celtic underworld. Made with copper
foil which suited the intricate shapes of the glass.

Three-dimensional panel

Antonio Dias Ribeiro
42 x 30 cm (17 x 12 in)
A fascinating piece in a frame of zinc, incorporating reclaimed broken wine bottles, small containers and several fused pieces of glass (glass melted in a kiln). The pieces were copper foiled and soldered together using wire and steel for extra strength.

Chinese music

Jo Wingrave
100 x 35 cm (39 x 14 in)
This panel consists of two layers of 3 mm (⅛ in) glass hand-painted with cold glass paint. The two pieces have been sandwiched together so the painting is on the inside within a frame of steel. Black relief outliner and red, gold and amber paint have been used. Designed for a Chinese library, the panel is based on modern and traditional Chinese music.

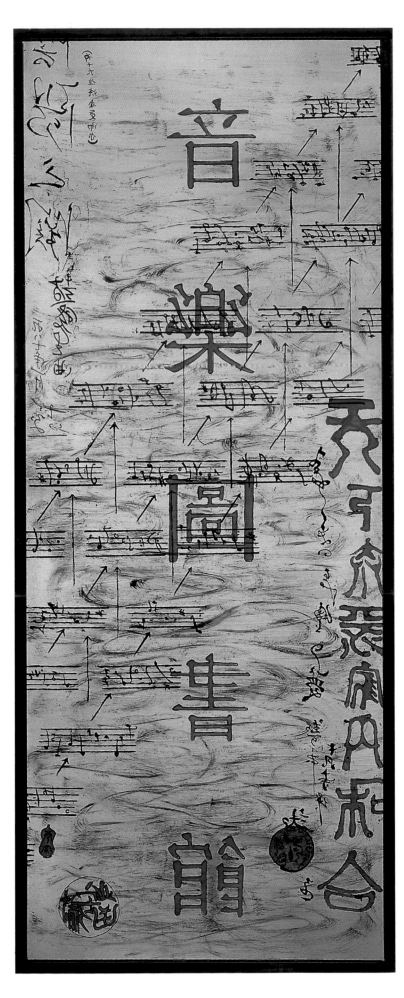

Bathroom window

Lynette Wrigley
47 x 78 cm (19 x 31 in)
An internal window installed in a partitioned wall. The design allows for the natural light source to penetrate the window and fill the dark interior. The window uses antique glass and is sandblasted and leaded.

Appliqué window

Antonio Dias Ribeiro
42 x 30 cm (17 x 12 in)
Appliqué offers a great deal of technical freedom when working in glass. This attractive window for a transom light above a door combines water glass and antique glass.

PATTERNS

The following patterns should be enlarged on a photocopier using its A4>A3 setting or its zoom facility set at 141%.

For the Sunflower appliqué below, make a photocopy as described above, then photocopy the photocopy using the same setting to produce a pattern of the right size.

Sunflower appliqué

(see page 22)

Decorative panel
(see page 28)

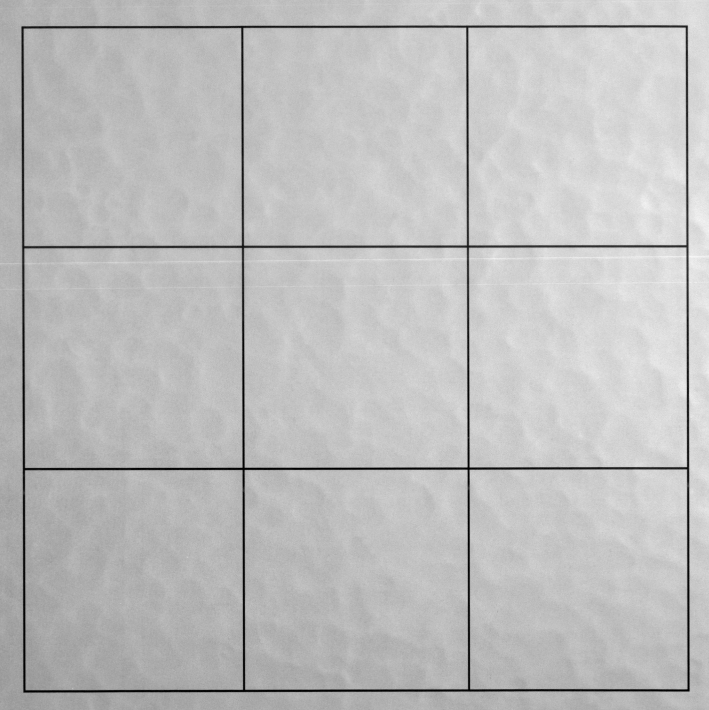

Pressed leaf mirror
(see page 30)

Autumn leaves
(see page 36)

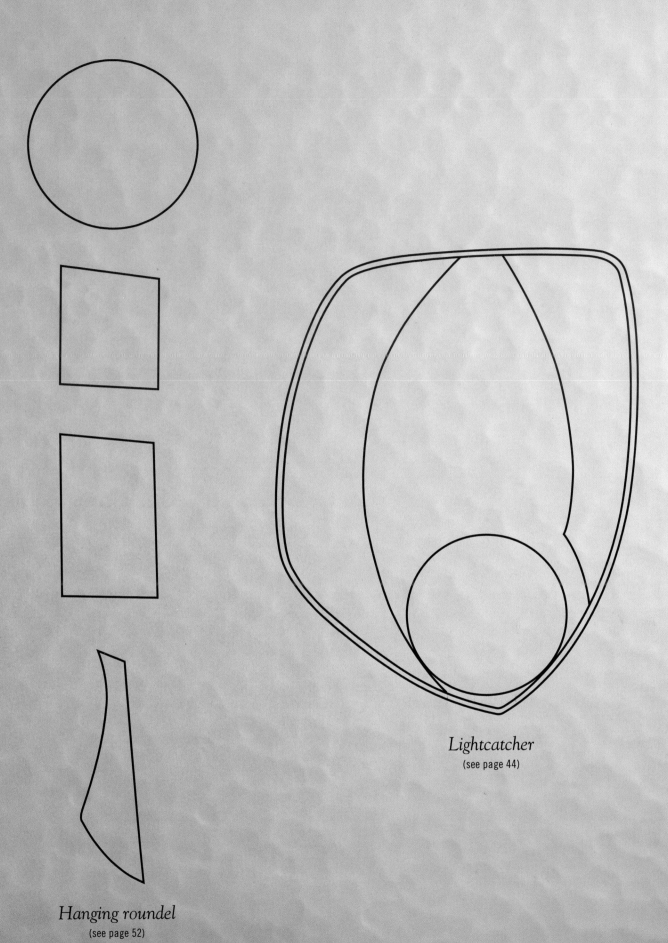

Lightcatcher
(see page 44)

Hanging roundel
(see page 52)

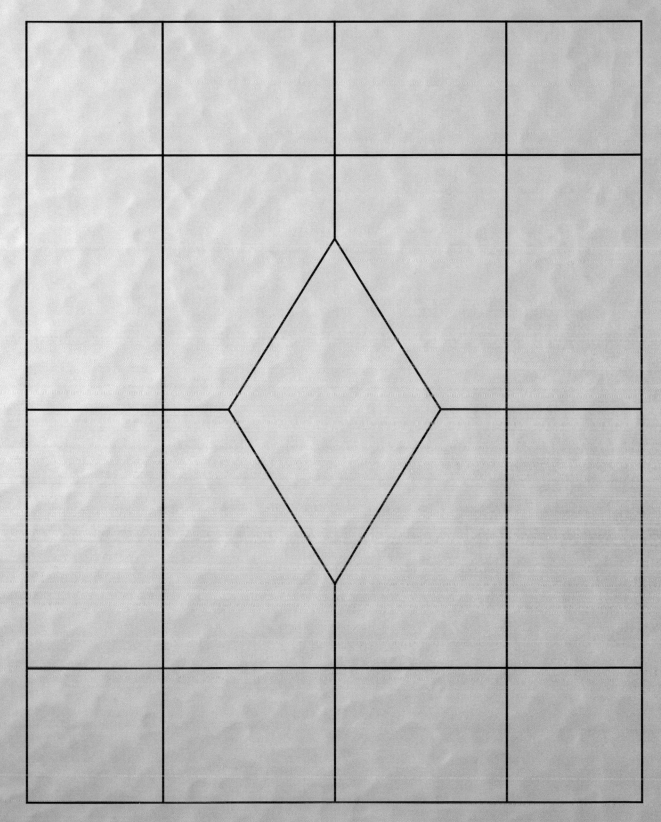

Leaded light
(see page 46)

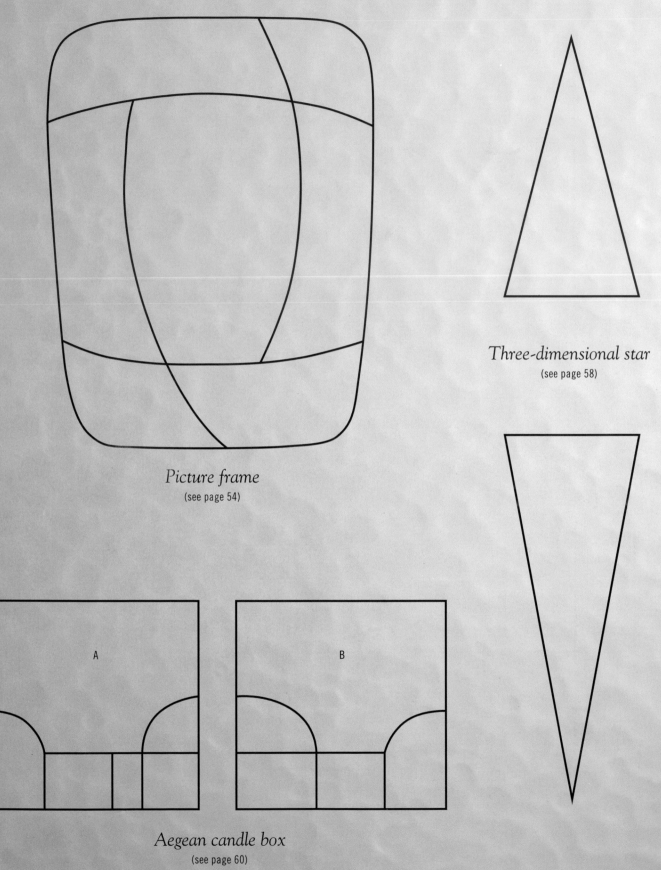

Picture frame

(see page 54)

Three-dimensional star

(see page 58)

Aegean candle box

(see page 60)

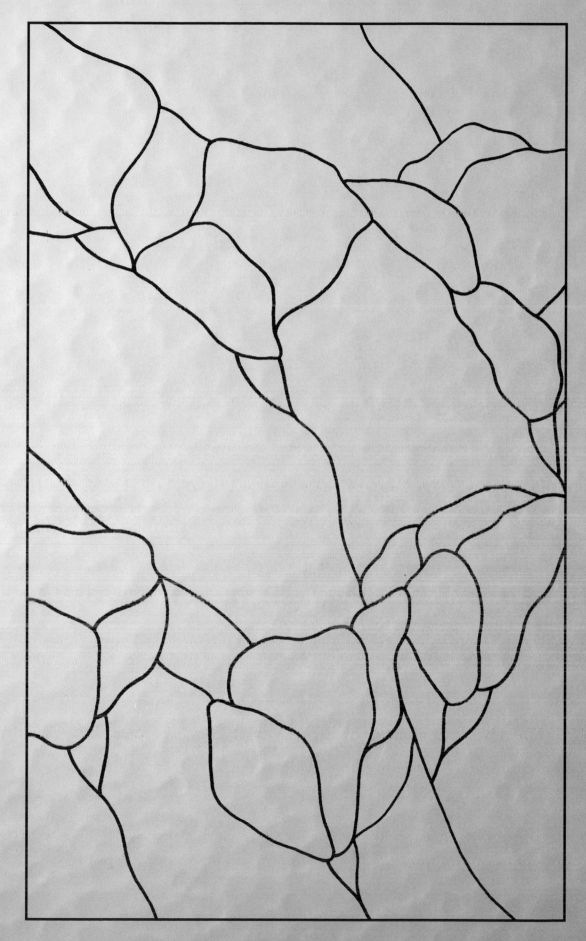

Tiffany window

(see page 62)

CONTRIBUTORS SUPPLIERS

UNITED KINGDOM

Janet Crook
Top flat
107 Seven Grove
Pontcanna
Cardiff CF1 9EQ
Tel: (01222) 223921

Antonio Dias Ribeiro
e.mail:
antonio.ribeiro@which.net

Deborah Flack
Krafty Designs
120 Holders Hill Road
London NW4 1LJ
Tel: 0956 492212

Anji Marfleet
Through The Looking Glass
12 Aspen Court
Emley
Nr Huddersfiled
West Yorkshire HD8 9RW
Tel: (01924) 840815

Helen Robinson
Oriel Stained Glass Studio
9 Ox Lane
Harpenden
Hertfordshire AL5 4HH
Tel: (01582) 764834

Richard Scowen
7 John Aird Court
Howley Place
London W2 1UY
Tel: 0171 2625142

Jo Wingrave
57a Victoria Road
Hendon
London
NW4 2RS

UNITED KINGDOM

Kansa Craft
The Old Flour Mill
Wath Road
Elsecar
Barnsley
S Yorks S74 8HW
Tel: 01226 747424

Lead & Light
35a Hartland Road
London NW1 4DB
Tel: (0171) 485 0997
*Glass and equipment by
mail order*

Fred Aldous
PO Box 135
37 Lever Street
Manchester 1
M60 1UX
Tel: (0161) 236 2477
*Jewellery findings and other
craft materials by mail order*

Specialist Crafts Ltd
PO Box 247
Leicester LE1 9QS
Tel: (0116) 251 0405
*Jewellery findings and other
craft materials by mail order*

SOUTH AFRICA

Leadgents Stained Glass
120 Queen Street
Kensington
Johannesburg
Tel: (011) 622-1302
Fax: (011) 616-1201

Glass Roots
226 Long Street
Cape Town
Tel: (021) 23-0552
Fax: (021) 557-3789

Glass Craft
Main Road
Lakeside
Cape Town
Tel: (021) 788-6329
Fax: (021) 788-6329

The Glass Studio
Medicine Forum
50 Bok Street
Welkom
Tel: (057) 352-3910

Meta Manufacturing
315 Umbilo Road
Umbilo
Durban
Tel: (031) 305-3307
Fax: (031) 305-3321

The Cozy Lamp Place
128 Kompanie Street
Sunnyside
Pretoria
Tel: (012) 344-1414
Fax: (012) 344-4290

AUSTRALIA

Australian Stained Glass Pty
  Ltd
39 Pyrmont Street
Pyrmont
NSW 2009
Tel: 02 9660 7444

Fitzroy Stained Glass
392 Queen's Parade
North Fitzroy
Victoria 3068
Tel: 03 9482 3622

The Stained Glass Centre
221 Hale Street
Petrie Terrace
Queensland 4000
Tel: 07 3369 0914

NEW ZEALAND

A Touch of Glass
670 Mt Albert Road
Royal Oak
Auckland
Tel: 09 625 9466

Chevalier Leadlights
44 Sunnyheights Road
Orewa
Tel: 09 426 3364 or
      09 489 5671

Glass Expressions
474 Dominion Road
Mt Eden
Auckland
Tel: 09 630 8103

Art Glass and Soul
3 Manukau Road
Epsom
Auckland
Tel: 09 520 1212

Leadlight Products (NZ) Ltd
Cnr Norton Road &
  Commerce Street
Hamilton
Tel: 0800 847 9213

INDEX

ACKNOWLEDGEMENTS

Thank you to Marc Gerstein of Lead & Light
(stained glass suppliers) in London for his
assistance and for the loan of all tools and
equipment. Many thanks also to Anji Marfleet,
Deborah Flack, Janet Crook, Helen Robinson,
Antonio Dias Ribeiro and Richard Scowen for
their contributions for the gallery pages.